BBC NATURE

Written by Sean Carson   Edited by Peter

Introduction	2	**World wildlife**	
Trees and woodland		Worldwide conservation	39
Oak tree	3	Observing and painting animals	40
Autumn: season of mists	4	Bengal tiger	41
Life on the woodland floor	6	Wolves	42
Tree diseases	7	Kangaroos	43
Trees in the park	8	American bison	44
Coniferous forests	9	Camels	45
Winter birds		**Wildlife in the city**	46
Feeding birds	10	**Nature in spring**	
Starlings	12	Springtime	48
Tufted ducks	14	**Reptiles in Britain**	
Winter thrushes	15	Adders and grass snakes	51
Mammals in Britain		Slow worms and lizards	52
Fallow deer	16	**Conservation issues**	
Red deer	17	Pollution problems	53
Otters	18	Hedgerows and roadsides	54
Grey seals	19	**Nature in summer**	
Foxes	20	Beetles	56
RSPB Bird quiz	22	Grasshoppers and crickets	57
Protecting our wildlife	23	Caterpillars and butterflies	58
Your body		Bumblebees	59
Skin	24	**Seaside**	
Heart	25	Herring gulls	60
Bones and teeth	26	Sand dunes	61
Freshwater life		Rock pools	62
Goldfish	29	Under the sea	64
Frogs and tadpoles	30	**Glossary**	
Newts	31	For help with some of the bigger words please see inside back cover!	
Pondlife	32		
Animal migration			
The salmon's journey	34		
The European eel	35		
Flight of the swift	36		
Warblers	38		

© Sean Carson and the British Broadcasting Corporation 1982
First published 1982
Published at the request of the School Broadcasting Council for the United Kingdom
by the British Broadcasting Corporation
35 Marylebone High Street, London W1M 4AA
Printed in England by Jolly & Barber Ltd, Rugby
ISBN 0 563 16520 0

Introduction

For parents and teachers

The broadcast connection
The BBC School Radio Nature series, currently taken by more than eleven thousand classes in the United Kingdom each week, goes out on Radio 4 (details in *Radio Times* or *BBC Annual Programme for Schools*). It is designed for children in the middle and upper end of the Primary School.

Topics in this book reflect those selected for broadcasting and a special set of Teacher's Notes is prepared each term with suggestions for follow-up activity and discovery.

Be nature detectives with Garry and Karen!
You can meet Garry, Karen and Uncle Douglas in our Nature programmes on Radio 4 (Schools service on VHF). Like all good naturalists they enjoy being outdoors – on the allotment in Manchester with their Dad or in the park. Sometimes they visit their Uncle Douglas who lives in the countryside of Shropshire. They keep pocket-sized notebooks and pencils with rubbers so they can jot down or draw things they see. Garry has a pair of old binoculars for birdwatching. Karen has a hand lens for the close examination of tiny creatures and she was given a small camera for her birthday.

Acknowledgements
The Editor would like to thank all those who participated in the preparation of this book. Special thanks go to the Picture Research Department of BBC Educational Publications, the commissioned artists and to the designer, Norman Brownsword.

The Royal Society for the Protection of Birds and the Young Ornithologists' Club
More and more people are taking an interest in wild birds and realise the need for their protection and conservation.

The Young Ornithologists' Club sends its members a colourful magazine six times a year. This contains interesting information about birds and other wildlife, quizzes, competitions and projects. There are members' courses and local and school YOC groups where members can meet.

For adults the Royal Society for the Protection of Birds is Europe's largest voluntary conservation organisation. It owns and manages over eighty reserves, offers a dynamic educational programme and carries out research, species protection and conservation. There are also local RSPB members' groups in many major towns. Most of the RSPB reserves may be visited by the public. Entry is free to RSPB and YOC members.

For full details of both organisations contact RSPB/YOC, The Lodge, Sandy, Beds SG19 2DL Telephone Sandy (0767) 80551.
Please send stamped, addressed envelopes. Now turn to page 22 for the RSPB Bird Quiz!

Young People's Trust for Endangered Species
YPTES was formed in January 1981 as the youth and educational division of the People's Trust for Endangered Species. It offers young people the opportunity to become part of a worldwide campaign to save endangered species and wild places. Special junior field study courses are organised for children aged 9–13 years often in conjunction with schools or youth groups such as Guides and Scouts.

YPTES organises fund-raising campaigns for special conservation projects. Operation Gorilla was launched thanks to the efforts of our 'Yippittees'. The People's Trust for Endangered Species has made major contributions to conservation at an International Whaling Conference. Money has been raised to fund scientific studies of whales which have increased man's knowledge of several species.

For fuller information of YPTES and the many services it offers write to: YPTES, 19 Quarry Street, Guildford, Surrey GU1 3EH Telephone Guildford (0483) 39600. *Please include stamped, addressed envelope.*

Did you know?
While the human population is likely to double during the next 35 years vast numbers of plants and animals will be lost ... and it is already being said that our world now loses one species of plant or animal each day!

Oak tree

Oaks are native to our islands. Sessile oaks, found mainly in the north and west, have no stalks to their acorns but have stalks on their leaves. Pedunculate oaks, found mainly in the south and east, are arranged the other way round! Can you work out which oak is shown in the photograph? There are three oaks introduced from other lands – the evergreen Holm oak, the Turkey oak with larger leaves and the Red oak.

It takes about a hundred years before an oak is fully grown. The tallest native oak is 41.5 metres high and the thickest, with a girth of 13.4 metres, is thought to be eight hundred years old. Robin Hood lived in an oakwood and King Charles II, as a prince, hid in an oak tree. Wooden ships were built of oak. Foresters selected trees with curved branches for the shipbuilders. Timber-framed houses were also made of oak, usually from trees grown close together to make long straight timbers. Oak bark, which contains an acid, was used to preserve leather.

You will recognise oaks by their acorns and lobed leaves, and in spring by twigs with clusters of buds at the tips. In May, tiny yellow catkins produce pollen. And in winter you will see the thick trunks with heavily scored bark and the 'zig-zag' branches.

Nearly three hundred different kinds of animals have been found living in or on oak trees. See what you can observe for your field notebook.

Aphids, like greenfly, will be sucking the sap from the leaves, and will be eaten in turn by ladybird larvae. You may find caterpillars of the oak-roller moth and the winter moth with great tits feeding on them at the rate of three hundred a day in summer! Other insect-eating birds will visit the tree, too. Can you recognise them in the picture below?

Under the tree will be millipedes, woodlice, snails, larvae and beetles of many sorts as well as shrews and woodmice. And of course, there will be the carnivores which live on small birds or mammals – kestrels, owls and foxes.

Autumn: season of mists

The poet John Keats described autumn in the famous line: 'Season of mists and mellow fruitfulness' (*Ode to Autumn*). It is the season of colour when the woods are filled with red and yellow light. The fruits of wild shrubs are red, black or orange and golden fields of corn fall under the combine harvesters.

There is great activity in nature. Animals feed plentifully and you will see more of them than at any other season. Migrating birds gather and resident birds are everywhere to be seen.

The weather is usually quite warm and sunny. And the air is still with morning and evening mists rising from the moist earth. We see these more often as sunrise is later and sunset earlier each day.

On 23 September, autumn officially begins. Light and darkness each last just twelve hours all over the world on that day. Gradually, in the northern half, daylight shortens until in Britain it reaches its shortest duration on 22 December, under 8 hours. Now winter begins. Remember that as it gets darker here it is getting lighter in the southern half of the world – in Australia for instance.

Next year's corn is often sown in autumn to allow it to grow a little before the winter and have a good start for the spring.

In autumn, as daylight shortens and growth slows down, leaves fall and fruits ripen.

Visit a wood or walk along a country hedge that the farmers may have left unspoiled. You will find many wild fruits easy to collect. Horse chestnuts or 'conkers' are still used in children's games. Others like hazel nuts, acorns or beech-mast may be found below their parent trees.

Some fruits still hang on trees like those in the pictures on these pages – do you recognise them? They are ash and sycamore. Look out for lime trees with their strange gliders!

On roadside verges, you may find dried pods with seeds inside, or flat seeds on the 'umbrellas' of wild parsnip or even on giant hogweeds, two metres tall! Poppies shake their tiny seeds out of holes in their 'pepper pot' heads. Rose hips and haws redden the hedges. And look out for elderberries, blackberries, bryony and other soft fruits. You could enter them all in your field notebook when you have managed to name them. Every year, there will be new shapes to puzzle over so you can extend your list.

You can also pick up coloured leaves that have fallen and arrange a lovely collage of every hue of red, yellow and brown. If you paint them with clear varnish they will keep all the winter on your bedroom wall.

Animals use autumn to prepare for the hardships of winter. Some, like the hedgehog, go to sleep (hibernate). Its heartbeat and bodily systems slow down and its temperature drops. The hedgehog can exist in this way, without food, until the spring. Some butterflies and other insects also hibernate in dry places. You may find one in your home.

If you come across a hedgehog in the autumn please do not make the mistake of bringing it indoors. It must be allowed to hibernate in the cold. Cover it with a wooden box to keep rain off. But tilt the box to allow the hedgehog to escape!

Other animals, like squirrels and jays, hide food in 'larders'. And in the winter they try to find it! Jays like burying acorns to eat later on but they often forget where they hid them. Many oak trees have grown up in this way!

Most animals, including birds, do not keep larders. They just eat as much as they can in the autumn when seeds and fruits are plentiful. When you see birds eating berries you may think they would be wiser to leave them for the winter. But the more they eat and store as fat in their bodies the better chance they have of surviving. They will still come out to find food whenever they can. Swallows and some other birds migrate in early autumn to find food in warmer countries.

Life on the woodland floor

Everyone loves walking through a wood and kicking up the deep carpet of leaves that covers the ground.

Naturalists divide woodland into 'layers' from the tops of the trees to the ground. First, there is the leaf canopy which is the very top layer where the leaves collect most sunlight. They use this energy to help make food.

Below that is the shrub layer which is between 2 and 5 metres from the ground. This is where enough light filters down to allow hawthorn, dogwood and other shrubs to grow. And below that is the field layer of plants which is between 15cm and 2 metres tall. Here you may find bracken and woodland flowers like bluebells and dog's mercury.

Finally, there is the ground layer where leaf litter lies and this is very important to all the plants in the wood including the trees themselves. It is rich in food for the soil. Leaf litter is a happy hunting ground for naturalists! In it leaves are decomposed or broken down to give up the goodness they contain to the soil. The roots of trees and other plants absorb this goodness again.

So leaf litter keeps up a regular food supply for all woodland plants and animals.

It is broken down by bacteria which are too small to see. You might be surprised at the number of fungi you can find in a wood in autumn. Other decomposers are small animals which rummage around leaf litter and eat it. You can have fun identifying them with this simple key.

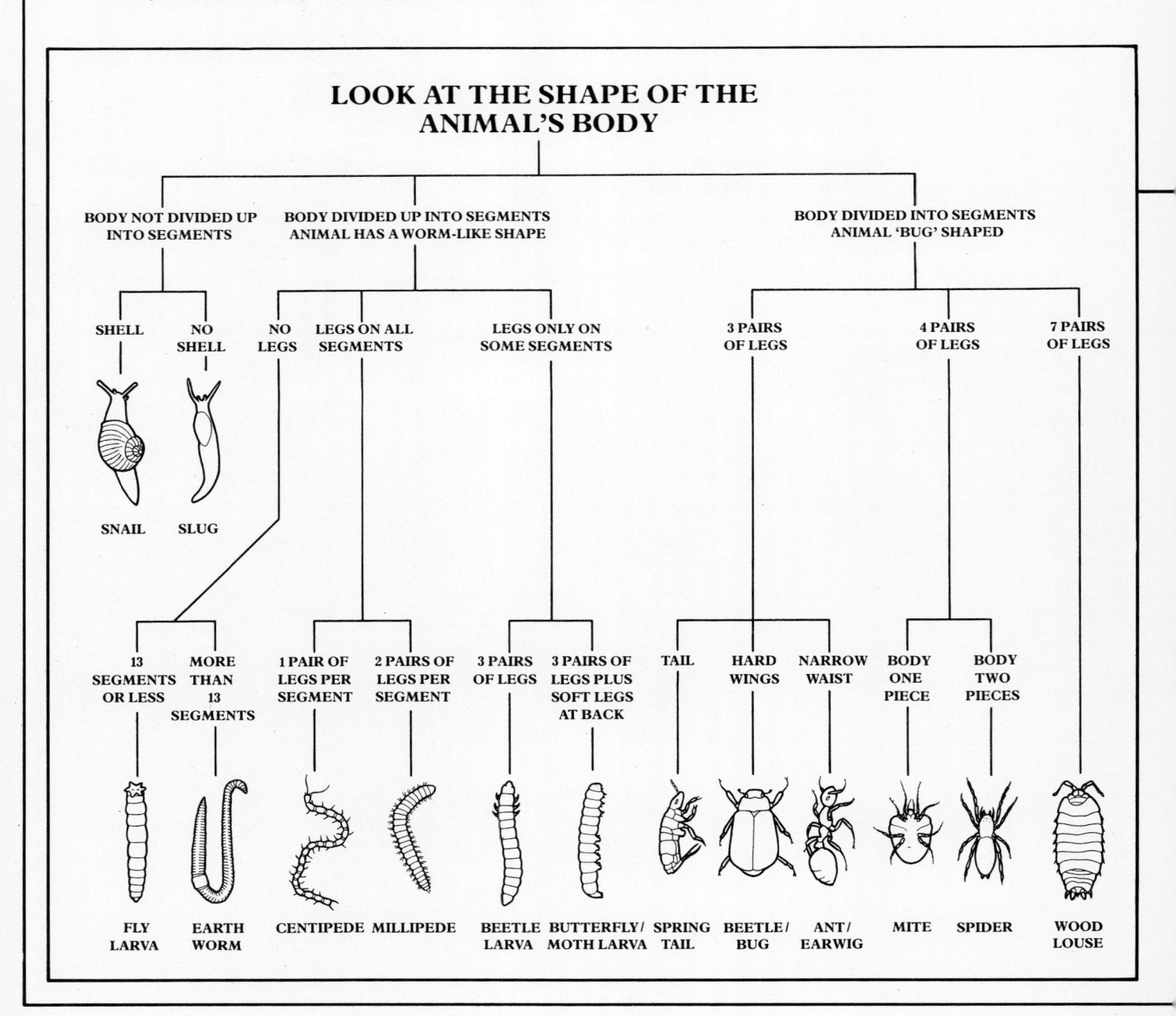

LOOK AT THE SHAPE OF THE ANIMAL'S BODY

- **BODY NOT DIVIDED UP INTO SEGMENTS**
  - SHELL — SNAIL
  - NO SHELL — SLUG
- **BODY DIVIDED UP INTO SEGMENTS — ANIMAL HAS A WORM-LIKE SHAPE**
  - NO LEGS
    - 13 SEGMENTS OR LESS — FLY LARVA
    - MORE THAN 13 SEGMENTS — EARTH WORM
  - LEGS ON ALL SEGMENTS
    - 1 PAIR OF LEGS PER SEGMENT — CENTIPEDE
    - 2 PAIRS OF LEGS PER SEGMENT — MILLIPEDE
  - LEGS ONLY ON SOME SEGMENTS
    - 3 PAIRS OF LEGS — BEETLE LARVA
    - 3 PAIRS OF LEGS PLUS SOFT LEGS AT BACK — BUTTERFLY/MOTH LARVA
- **BODY DIVIDED INTO SEGMENTS — ANIMAL 'BUG' SHAPED**
  - 3 PAIRS OF LEGS
    - TAIL — SPRING TAIL
    - HARD WINGS — BEETLE/BUG
    - NARROW WAIST — ANT/EARWIG
  - 4 PAIRS OF LEGS
    - BODY ONE PIECE — MITE
    - BODY TWO PIECES — SPIDER
  - 7 PAIRS OF LEGS — WOOD LOUSE

Tree diseases

Dutch Elm disease is the most spectacular disaster to strike trees in this century. It is estimated that in 1960 there were twenty five million elm trees in the Midlands and southern Britain. Most had been planted in hedges. At a century old they often reached 30 metres high and were a magnificent feature of the landscape.

The disease broke out in Britain around 1970 and has continued to spread since. More than half of the elm trees in England have already been destroyed. The disease is caused by a fungus with strange connections! Beetles carry it into the tree and it can feed on their droppings. You can see elm bark beetles in the picture (*bottom right*).

The adult beetles are brown insects 3–4mm long. In summer, they fly to the trees and burrow under the bark. Here they mate and the female lays eggs. These become larvae as shown in the picture on the right.

Their food is the tree sap and the fungus itself. To feed they tunnel under the bark and into the living wood and the fungus prevents food from being carried to and from the leaves. The larvae eventually become pupae and the following year they emerge as adult beetles flying off to other trees with their deadly fungus.

Meanwhile the tree begins to die. Groups of dead branches appear and the leaves grow yellow and wither in the summer. Eventually the whole tree dies.

Different bark beetles attack other trees too. Each sort has its own tree and special fungus. Beech trees are also attacked by other fungal diseases (*Picture, far left*).

Coniferous woodlands (*see page 9*) may suffer from insect pests. So the Forestry Commission sprays large areas of woodland from the air against the destructive pine weevil larvae and other harmful insects.

Trees in the park

Your local park will probably have a variety of trees. You will quickly learn to recognise them and your field notebook could contain sketches of leaves, twigs and fruits. Take the oak for instance. When was it planted? Is there a plaque? Is it sessile or pedunculate? (*See page 3*). Maybe it is a Holm oak with glossy evergreen leaves, or a Turkey oak with very large leaves. Perhaps it is a Red oak which turns a lovely autumn colour.

You cannot mistake a silver birch with its white bark and gentle, weeping branches. But in your park you may have the rarer 'Paper birch' with whiter bark. Red Indians, in North America, used it to build their canoes!

Horse chestnuts may have red or white flowers but they are not natives of Britain. About three hundred years ago they were one of many new plants to be introduced.

Plane trees are popular in towns with their clusters of round fruits.

Look out for the conifers (*see page 9*) which are usually evergreen in winter. There is at least one that is not. Can you name them? Forests of Scots pine used to cover the Highlands of Scotland until they were nearly destroyed for timber two hundred years ago. Scots pines live for about one hundred and fifty years. Their bark is rough and they also make a sticky resin which has a lovely pine scent. You may also find trees introduced from other lands such as the one named Wellingtonia. This pine, from America, became popular with the Victorians. It is very tall, straight and pointed with a curious spongy bark. The giant Sequoias (redwoods), the oldest and tallest trees in the world, are related to it. Some grow 100 metres high.

Find out if there is a Ginkgo tree in your park. Or a cedar of Lebanon or a monkey puzzle tree. You can visit other parks, too, and make your own list of trees.

Coniferous forests

Forty years to grow; forty seconds to cut down! During the First World War (1914–1918) Britain cleared enormous areas of forest for timber. In 1919, the Government set up the Forestry Commission to replace them. Now forests cover about one tenth of the land – more so than at any time since the Normans! The Commission generally plants trees that grow quickly such as Sitka spruce, Corsican pine, Norway spruce and Douglas fir.

Seedlings are planted in nursery beds. When they are two years old and about 0.5 metres tall they are moved out to their final forest row and are planted close together.

Some years later, when the trees have made a thick wood and are about 8 metres tall, the forester thins out many of them. Then more light gets into the wood allowing many new plants and animals to find a home. After a further twenty years the trees, at about 20 metres tall, are ready for felling. The timber, as shown here, may be used for posts or building joists. Soon afterwards new seedlings are planted in their places. After the trees have been felled the area may be invaded by wild flowers. Conifer forests now cover remote moors, mountainsides and land otherwise of little value. Some naturalists do not like them as they do not contain the variety of wildlife that lives in natural woodland. But red squirrels, badgers, weasels, stoats and small mammals like voles and shrews all live there. Rare polecats would not have survived in Wales but for protection in these forests. Muntjac, fallow and roe deer all live in forests in the south. Crossbills and the goldcrests (*shown here*) and jays and woodpeckers are all to be found. There are many fungi, dragonflies, moths and butterflies too.

Naturalists should find coniferous forests full of interest. Keep your notebook, binoculars and camera handy. You may find that most of the birds are high in the trees and the deer are very shy.

Feeding birds

Wild birds in Britain are up against problems that we have made for them. Often we destroy their homes when we build new roads, houses and factories, and in the countryside new ways of farming can destroy their food plants or insects.

Small nature reserves can be made in town or country gardens or in open spaces in towns. If you have a garden you can encourage birds to come to it. And you can grow useful shrubs with berries or leave untidy places and hedges for birds to hide in.

You will need a good bird-table. This must be cat proof and hung from a bracket or placed on top of an unclimbable pole. It is a good idea to have a roof over it but this is not essential. Because so many birds feed on particular foods you should give them a range of food holders. Tits, which eat insects in trees in summer, will come to a winter bird-table for fat, suet or peanuts. They are very acrobatic and can feed from hanging wire baskets or half a coconut where other birds cannot perch.

Greenfinches and robins will come to your bird-table. Finches like an assortment of seeds and small nuts in nets or wire holders. Robins are easy to please. They can be taught to eat from your hand and they like crumbled biscuits or cereals. Wrens, however, are very timid. They may appear on your table if there are no other birds about and eat small seeds or crumbs or tiny pieces of cheese. But they prefer to stay under cover near a hedge.

Thrushes, including blackbirds and the migrating redwings and fieldfares, like to eat fallen apples, fruit or berries. Blackbirds will land on the bird-table although they dislike going under a roof. They can be quite aggressive towards other birds. You will certainly have house sparrows – and tree sparrows if you live in the country. They are delightful to watch as they preen, chatter and quarrel for food.

Starlings are sure to come too. But they are apt to clear the table in a few beakfuls and gobble food that would last other birds all day!

It is fun to record which birds come to feed. So make sure that your field notebook is at hand. This is a good way to study birds as they are moving about quite close to you for some time. Dunnocks will arrive and you may be visited by woodpeckers, treecreepers, or nuthatches. Collared doves will search for their special needs, not so much on the bird-table but in the rest of the garden. Pied wagtails may strut over your lawn, too, and all these are worth recording

It is very important that the supply of food should be regular. Keep this going whatever the weather as birds come to rely on it. You can buy a regular amount of bird food from most pet shops – either loose or in packets. Table scraps are usually fine but avoid boiled vegetables or anything with salt in it, or white bread. And please make sure that you do not feed birds with salted peanuts. Any brown bread or cake should be soaked in water and squeezed and not put out dry. Don't forget a bowl of water will you? Birds always need water and if there is a frost they may not be able to find any nearby.

Starlings

You won't mistake starlings! They visit your garden or street most days, whether you live in the north or the south, often chasing away smaller birds.

You may not think them very attractive when they steal the food on the bird-table from tits and robins. But take another look at them! Starlings have a shiny, purple-green colour like shot-silk to their blue-black coats and showy, speckled breasts. Their song may not sound as beautiful as that of the thrush or blackbird, but starlings are clever mimics. If you listen, you will hear squeaks, whistles, snatches of songs and even imitations of human voices, car noises or hammering!

It is interesting to observe carefully which birds starlings manage to frighten off and which ones stand up to them. Why not keep your field notebook handy by the window overlooking the bird-table and list (1) those birds that fly away as soon as a starling appears on the table (2) those that stay until the starling threatens them (3) those that try to hold their own but are defeated, and (4) those that stay in spite of the starling's threats? You may find that some smaller birds stand up for themselves quite successfully.

Although starlings are aggressive, even to each other, they gather in flocks to roost at night. In winter, these roosts may be 30 kilometres or more from their feeding grounds and may hold half a million to a million birds. Winter roosts are often found in city centres where the temperature may be 5 or 6 degrees (C) higher than in the surrounding countryside. At this time, our local starlings may be joined by millions of continental birds escaping Europe's colder weather. Starling roosts can be a problem – fouling buildings and pavements, or destroying woodland undergrowth.

A local summer roost may be small enough for you to observe and count the inhabitants. The birds always use the same flight paths. A group of birdwatchers should observe for about an hour at about dusk. But don't count every bird, count just the number that fly in on each path in, say, three minutes. You may have to count them in batches of fives or tens. Starlings will continue to come in at about the same rate until they have all arrived. Check the time and see if you can calculate the total.

Starlings feed on insects, particularly leatherjackets which are the larvae of craneflies or 'daddy longlegs'. But if need be, they can eat almost anything, including fruit, berries or scraps. They nest in holes that they find ready made in trees, walls, or rocks and the young are hatched in April or May. You will see them worrying their parents for food until about ten days after they leave the nest when they quickly become independent.

Tufted ducks

Tufted ducks are diving ducks that can swim under water whereas ducks like mallards just 'up-end' themselves. This means that tufted ducks can feed from much deeper water. The male tufted ducks, the drakes, are purplish-black with white sides. They have feathery tufts at the backs of their heads that will not lie down! The females are dull brown with pale sides and with smaller tufts. Tufted ducks feed on the little animals that live among the submerged plants — water snails, shrimps and small water insects.

Diving ducks do not often come on land. If they do they seem very clumsy because their short legs and webbed feet are placed far back on their bodies to help in swimming. They take off from water with a long 'run' to get up speed and for this reason they cannot use very small ponds or streams. Mallards, on the other hand, take off very steeply. They can escape from a tiny pond and yet clear tall shrubs. In the picture you see tufted ducks taking off and landing.

Tufted ducks are mainly visitors coming here in the winter from northern Europe and Siberia where the ice has covered their feeding lakes. They can be seen on any large area of water such as a lake in the town park, a reservoir or at the sea shore. However, since about one hundred and fifty years ago they have begun to stay the whole year in the British Isles. And they are increasing in number so some now breed here regularly. To nest, they need good cover at the edge of the water — reeds or rushes for example. Here the female hatches up to a dozen ducklings. After nesting, tufted ducks join up in large flocks for most of the year.

It is interesting to observe your local lake, in a park perhaps, and to note the dates when tufted ducks appear and leave, and whether any stay to breed. Try timing their dives with a watch with a second hand (or a digital watch). How long do you think they can stay under water? Will it be in seconds or minutes?

Winter thrushes

There are six different birds in the thrush family – song thrushes, mistle thrushes, blackbirds and ring ouzels, fieldfares and redwings. The first three are residents so they stay in our country all the year round. The ring ouzel is a summer visitor to the coasts or to high moorland, and fieldfares and redwings visit us only for the winter.

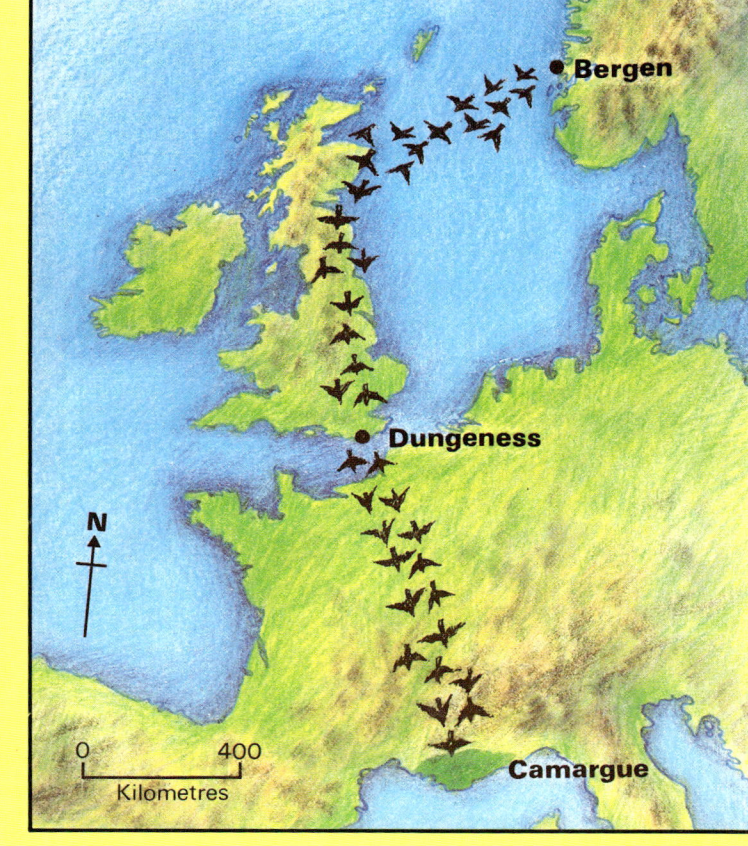

Although all thrushes eat snails as well as berries and fruit, they also feed on soil animals such as earthworms, leather jackets and beetles.

When the ground is frozen in winter they suffer badly. This may be the reason why even our resident thrushes move southwards in the winter and song thrushes from northern Europe migrate here across the North Sea. But many die from starvation on this journey.

Redwings (*below, left*) and fieldfares (*below, right*) are better fliers than song thrushes. They move south in winter from northern Europe as the ground freezes. Both these thrushes can be seen in open fields, playing fields or in town parks. They also come into gardens with large lawns to eat insects, fallen apples or berries. Fieldfares stay in large flocks. They have blue-grey heads and rumps and are larger than song thrushes. Redwings are smaller and can be recognised by their white eyestripes as well as by the reddish patches on their sides.

Neither of these birds sings like a song thrush. Sometimes the sad, high-pitched notes of redwing calls can be heard as they pass overhead. You can count redwings or fieldfares in a flock in an open field. The usual method is to count ten and then estimate how many 'tens' there are in the total flock. (*Left*) The winter journey of redwings.

Fallow deer

Wild fallow deer are found over many parts of England. There are also some in Wales, Ireland and Scotland. They live in small groups of five to fifty head and move over wide stretches of countryside to browse on twigs, leaves, grass and green corn.

The mating season or 'rut' is in October. Bucks (the male deer) fight with their antlers which are cast off and regrown each year (*see right*). The winners collect a herd of does (the females) for mating. They guard the herds through the winter and spring.

In May, the does separate and go off to seek a hiding place. Usually a single fawn is born to each doe early in June. It is well camouflaged and stands very still when the mother has to feed. The fawn is usually feeding for itself by early spring of the next year.

Watch out for fallow deer in the countryside. Look for their tracks at woodland edges.

Many centuries ago, fallow deer were introduced into Britain for hunting.

Red deer

Red deer are the largest native wild animals living in Britain. Stags, or male deer, can measure 1.4 metres high at the shoulder. About 250,000 red deer roam the Scottish Highlands. Some live in the English Lake District and on Exmoor, but they are no longer found wild in the rest of the country. At one time, they were widespread but hunting and the cutting down of woods over the centuries has driven them to more remote areas. Red deer are still hunted on Exmoor whilst some farmers in Scotland are trying to rear them for meat.

They eat beechmast, acorns and chestnuts in the autumn but they mainly browse on the young shoots of shrubs and trees. In doing so they prevent tree seedlings from growing. So foresters build tall deer fences round their plantations to keep them out.

Stags grow huge spiked antlers each year. The number of spikes increases so that a seven year old stag has a magnificent spread. Red deer are reddish-brown in summer with a thick, darker coat in winter. Under their tails are white patches which other deer can see from a long distance. Can you think why this is an advantage to red deer?

Stags and hinds (the females) keep in separate groups until the mating or 'rutting' season in autumn. Then the stags roar out their challenges across the hills and fight furiously to gather their own groups of hinds. Those with the greatest antlers often win, before they become too old. Antlers also help to protect the deer from hounds or other enemies.

In winter, the deer come down from the mountains or high hills.

In spring, the hinds of about three years of age seek out hiding places and give birth to their single calves. The fawns have pale spots at first.

Otters

Your best chance of seeing an otter is at a wildlife park or at the Otter Trust. Few wild otters remain in most parts of Britain. Perhaps you could find out why? Now, in England, Scotland and Wales they are protected by law.

Otters are mammals which can live in water but breathe air. Their chocolate brown fur is waterproof and they can close their eyes and nostrils underwater. A lot of their time is spent playing, sliding, diving and somersaulting.

In the wild otters hunt at night. During the day they lie up in burrows in the bank called holts. Mating takes place in the autumn and the bitch gives birth in April or May to two, three or four cubs. These are born with closed eyes and are suckled in the holt until eight weeks old. At about three months they begin to hunt for fish, or shellfish in river estuaries. The father, or dog otter, leaves them but the bitch looks after them until the following April.

Grey seals

Colonies of Atlantic grey seals live mainly on the western coasts or islands of the British Isles. However, the best known group lives in the east on the Farne Islands off the Northumbrian coast. Seals eat fish and have been persecuted as they are not popular with local fishermen.

Grey seals come ashore in autumn and the females, or cows, give birth to a single pup. One bull seal may have many cows and guards them fiercely in the packed colony. The pups feed on their mothers' rich milk and for three weeks have pure, white fur.

Grey seals are clumsy on land but are wonderful swimmers. They use their powerful hind flippers to propel themselves through the water and can stay below for up to half an hour. Seals, like all sea mammals, keep warm with an extra layer of fat below the skin called blubber.

Grey seals measure up to 2.4 metres and are larger than the Common seal which is also found off our coasts.

Foxes

Foxes are mainly carnivorous. They eat hedgehogs, voles and other rodents, also small birds, beetles and even moths, earthworms and slugs. In winter and spring, they eat young hares and rabbits, whilst in autumn they add fruit to their diet.

You may see foxes in towns when they raid dustbins at night. But their traditional home is the open countryside. You will not often see foxes in the daytime but you may hear them at night or see them in the headlights of a car. You can distinguish their tracks in soft mud or recognise their droppings and you can remember their scent once you have smelt it. These signs are all worth entering in your field notebook.

Foxes mate in mid-winter and the cubs are born usually in March or April. The female, or vixen, has a litter of four or five cubs. She will already have found an earth (the fox's burrow) in which to live. The young are born with their eyes closed but with woolly coats. The eyes open at ten days and the cubs stay below ground suckling their mother for about a month. Then they come

Foxes are territorial animals, each with its own hunting area. In any district there may be a dominant fox which none of the others dares to fight. At night foxes warn others off by 'screaming'. This is a very eerie sound in the countryside. They mark their territories with their scent glands or by leaving droppings or urinating at fixed points. So the young find their own territories where they will not be challenged. For this they may have to travel up to forty kilometres.

Foxes have very acute senses of smell, hearing and sight and know their district in great detail. They see any movement, any new shape or shadow and can hear breathing. So it is very hard to approach them.

On the continent of Europe, foxes and other mammals may carry rabies. This is a disease and it can be given to humans. It causes madness and death. So far the disease has not spread to Britain. Can you find out about our quarantine laws?

up to play at the entrance. Cubs have an instinct to hunt and from an early age play at pouncing on their prey.

At six weeks the vixen may move to a separate earth, although she will often visit the cubs. Sometimes the whole family may move. Probably this is because they are such untidy animals. They quickly foul up their earth and its surroundings. The dog fox, the father, often lives apart yet some have been seen taking food to the vixen. The young grow up until about September when they begin to move away.

Bird quiz

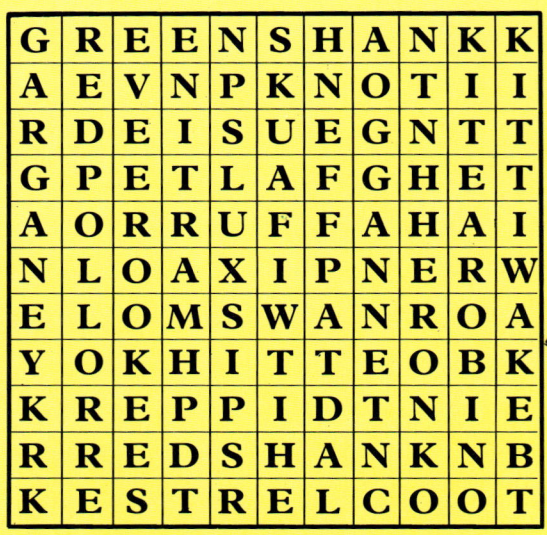

G	R	E	E	N	S	H	A	N	K	K
A	E	V	N	P	K	N	O	T	I	I
R	D	E	I	S	U	E	G	N	T	T
G	P	E	T	L	A	F	G	H	E	T
A	O	R	R	U	F	F	A	H	A	I
N	L	O	A	X	I	P	N	E	R	W
E	L	O	M	S	W	A	N	R	O	A
Y	O	K	H	I	T	T	E	O	B	K
K	R	E	P	P	I	D	T	N	I	E
R	R	E	D	S	H	A	N	K	N	B
K	E	S	T	R	E	L	C	O	O	T

The names of twenty birds regularly seen in Britain are hidden in this square. Can you find them all? They have been written in straight lines forwards, backwards, up and down and diagonally!

Can you identify eight birds mixed up below?
Top bird: 1 Tail, 2 Wings and legs, 3 Head and neck.
Lower bird: 4 Head, 5 Neck, 6 Body and wing, 7 Feet, 8 Tail.

Try to unscramble the birds I saw on this birdwatching trip.

'Last summer a fabulous day was spent watching birds at the famous RSPB reserve at Minsmere, Suffolk. From a hiding place overlooking the muddy scrape I saw thirty **CEATVOS**, some with young. There were also **LESHCUDK**, a **NEHOR** and a **PINES** with large numbers of **KACBL DEADHE SLLUG** and **CHANDIWS RENTS**. Most exciting of all was a **LIBONPOLS**. From the reeds, in which several **REDABED ITTS** were seen flying about, I was lucky to hear a **BRENTIT** booming. A **DERE RAWBLEW** was seen feeding a baby **UOCOCK**, and I was thrilled to observe a **SHARM RIRAHER** hunting.'

Find the path through the maze. The arrow shows you where to start.

See inside back cover for the names of the eight birds.

Using crayons, felt-tipped pens or paints colour in the bird according to the instructions. What bird is it?

Crown, nape, neck   blue-grey
Chin, throat, cheek, breast   pink
Back   brown
Rump   dull green
Beak, belly   pale grey
Legs, wings, tail   brownish-black
Wing bars, outer tail feathers   white

Protecting our wildlife

Although we often take them for granted, wild animals and plants and the places they live in need our protection.

The *Nature Conservancy Council* is the organisation set up by Parliament to protect Britain's wildlife and wild places. It manages over one hundred and eighty National Nature Reserves in England, Scotland and Wales.

More and more people are taking an interest in the wildlife of our towns and cities and nature reserves are being created on waste ground for local people to study and enjoy. Foxes *(see page 20)* have moved into some towns and cities to feed on waste food and scraps.

Even badgers *(see below)* are known to visit people's gardens regularly. They are seldom seen during the day, emerging at dusk in search of food, their favourite being earthworms. They also eat mice and voles, wasps' nests and other pests and so are welcomed by foresters. Many years ago they were persecuted and badger-digging was considered a 'sport' but since 1973 badgers have been protected by law.

The wild cat *(see below)* is another native mammal which now receives some protection from a recent law – *The Wildlife & Countryside Act 1981*. It can still be killed if, for instance, a landowner decides that it has become a pest. However, he cannot do this in any of the very cruel ways that have been used in the past. He is no longer allowed to put down certain kinds of snare, trap or poison.

In recent years, the wildcat has begun to increase its numbers. Although it is still found mostly in the Scottish Highlands it is now beginning to live further south.

Alas, the red squirrel our native species, has gone down in numbers. Now it is found mainly in East Anglia, North Wales, Northern England, Scotland and Ireland.

The Wildlife & Countryside Act 1981 gives legal protection to forty four wild animals. These include all fifteen British species of bats and several rare insects, spiders and snails. This Act also gives special protection to sixty two species of wild plants, including eight orchids and indeed it is illegal to uproot any wild plant without the landowner's permission.

The laws which help to protect birds are quite complicated. However, it can be said that all wild birds are now well protected. It is an offence to disturb or take a nest if it is still being used by the birds.

Skin

Skin covers you all over. As you grow, it grows too – unlike the skin of a caterpillar which has to be shed. The drawing shows just a tiny piece of skin made to look large. There are four layers. On the inside is a layer of fat to keep you warm. Next, there is an inner layer and on top of that a thinner, outer layer. On the surface is a layer of dead skin cells. Did you know that your skin is always wearing off on top and being renewed from inside? The dead skin hardens on our heels or on the tips of your fingers. Your nails are made of the same material. Other animals have claws or hooves made of it. Does it hurt a horse to have its shoes nailed on? Hair is another special 'dead' material. Your skin is covered by fine hairs. But on your head they grow much longer and closer together.

Each hair starts in a tiny gland and grows through the skin layers. All mammals have hair and in many it grows into a warm coat of fur. Human beings, as we know them, probably began life in Africa and did not need such a covering. When they spread to colder places they had to wear animal skins to keep warm.

Skin also helps you to keep your temperature at about the same level. All mammals control their temperatures. If you get too warm your sweat glands push out drops of warm water. The water evaporates and its heat escapes. This results in your cooling down. It happens all the time but you only notice it when you have got very hot. Perhaps when you have been running fast. In a normal day, you lose about half a litre of water by sweating. Dogs have no sweat glands so they pant a lot to cool down.

Elephants pump blood through their large ears to lose heat. The ears are like enormous radiators.

When you are cold you get 'gooseflesh'. Little skin muscles pull on your hairs. In other mammals this results in a thicker coat but you have not enough hair to make it work.

Skin has nerve endings in the inner layer. Through these you feel heat, cold, light touches or heavy touches and pain.

Bacteria cannot get through the skin – though they may live on the outside unless it is frequently washed!

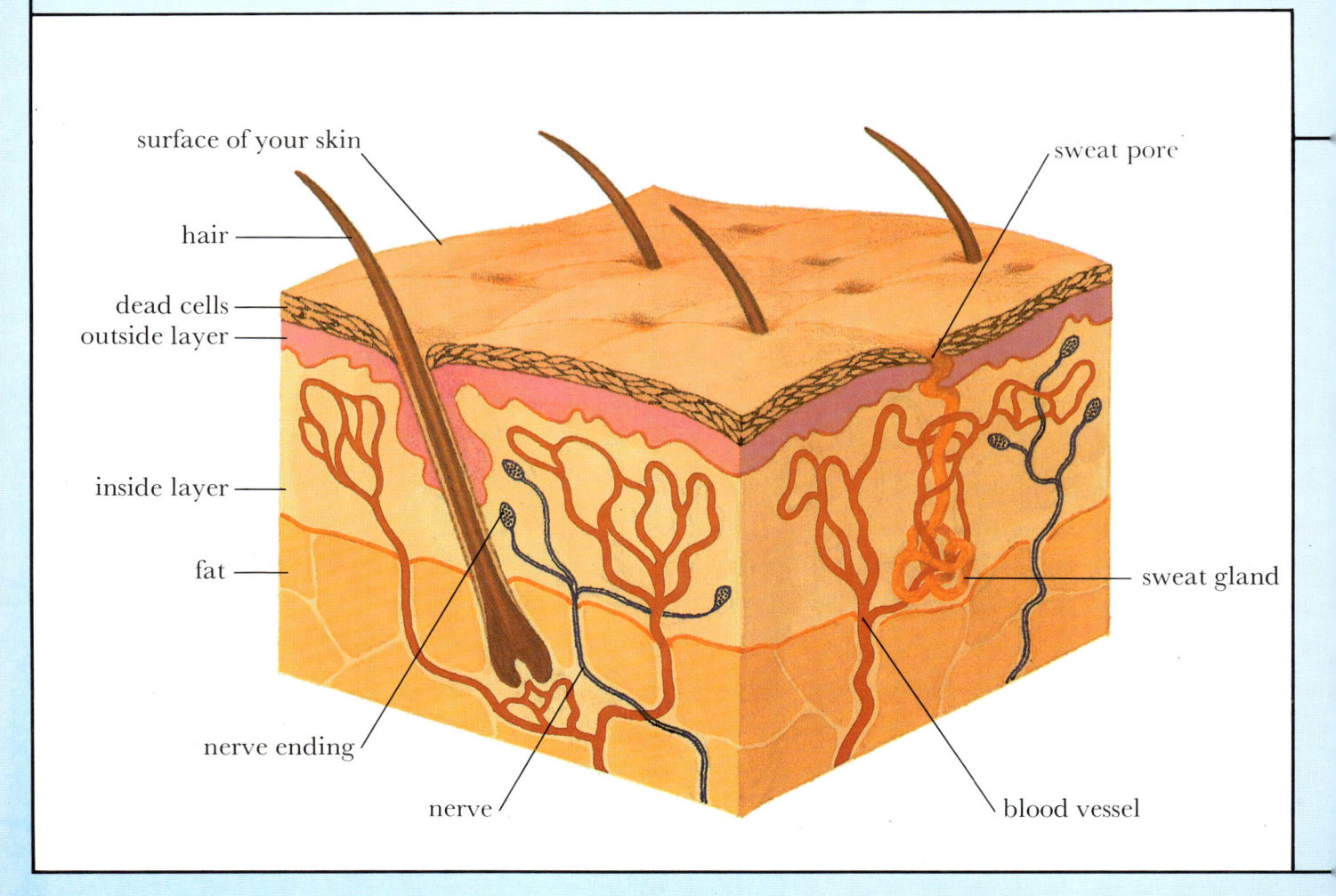

Heart

Your heart is really two pumping stations joined together to pump blood around your body. Each pump has two spaces. One is to receive blood coming into it (auricle) and another with strong muscles to pump it out again (ventricle). They are joined by valves that only allow blood through in one direction. When your heart beats, what you feel is the alternate 'squeeze' and 'relax' as the muscular pumps work.

We can follow the journey of the bloodstream. Imagine the route as a figure of '8' with the pumping heart at the crossway in the centre. Blood is pumped round and round the '8' all the time, never stopping. One half of the '8' leads through the lungs to collect oxygen and comes back. The other half leads round the body and returns.

One of the pumps pushes blood from the heart to the body (red) and the other receives and pushes it to the lungs again (maroon).

Blood travels from the heart through pipes called arteries. Gradually these divide into narrower pipes and finally into millions of tiny capillaries which give blood to every body cell. On its way back, the blood travels from the capillaries to wider pipes called veins. And finally into a wider vein and then to the heart. The blood has lost all its oxygen so must be pumped to the lungs. While it is in the tiny capillaries of the lungs blood collects oxygen breathed in and becomes bright red. But when it reaches the capillaries of the body it releases oxygen to each cell and loads up with carbon dioxide. It loses its bright red colour and carries the carbon dioxide back to the lungs where you breathe it out. At the lungs it collects more oxygen. At the same time, the transport service of the blood has other jobs to do. It collects and delivers food for the cells of the body. Poisonous waste is picked up and dropped off at the kidneys. Eventually that is passed away as urine. White cells which fight against disease germs are carried to wherever they are needed to conduct their battles. Regular exercise keeps the heart healthy!

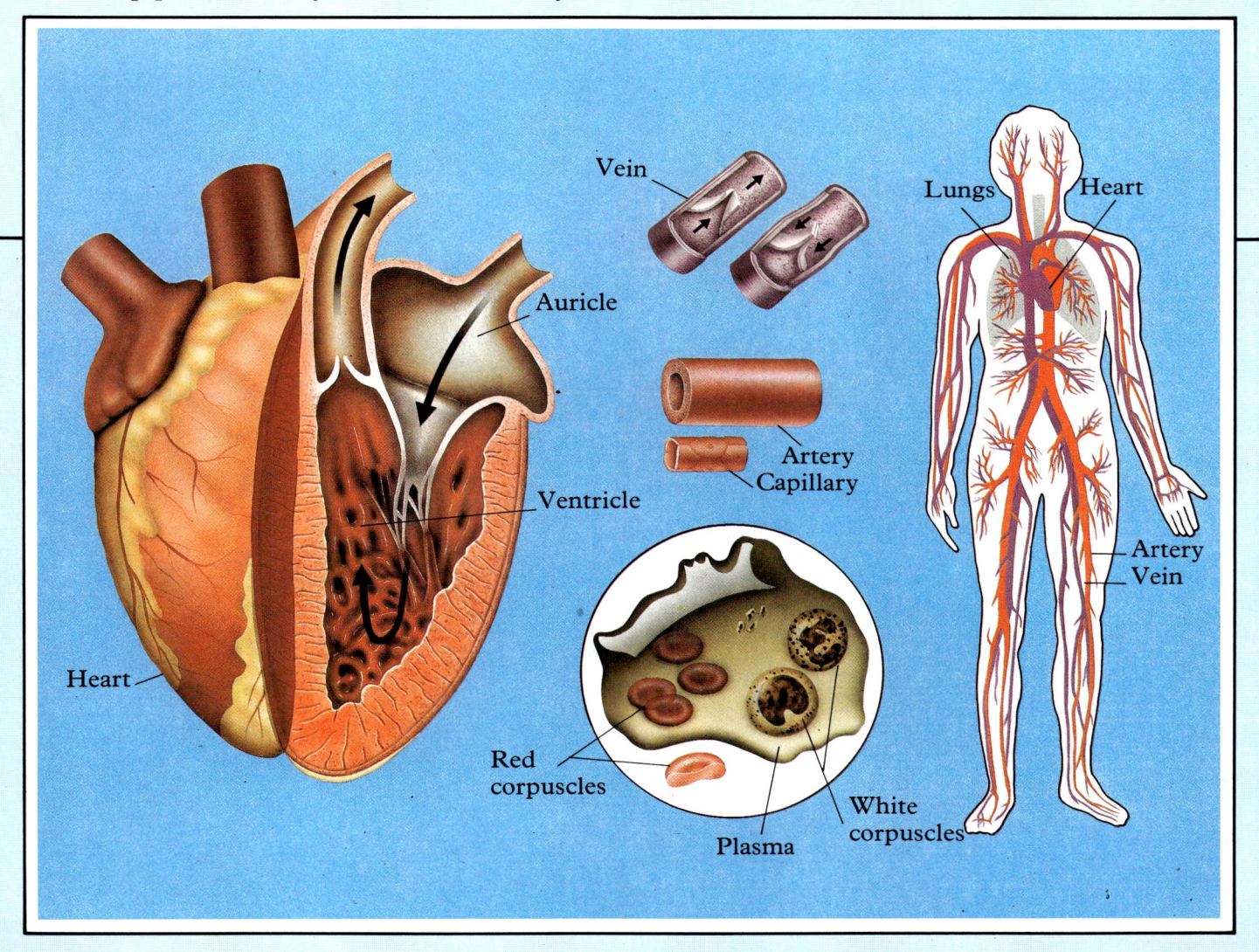

Bones and teeth

Some animals have no bones. Can you think of any? Others, like the crab, have an outside shell. We have a bony skeleton *inside* our bodies with the bones arranged equally either side of a backbone. The backbone is actually a long rod of separate, small bones called vertebrae. These fit together so as to allow the backbone to bend. Try to find out what is the special word for backboned animals.

Bones provide anchors for muscles. We could not move without muscles which are fixed at each end to firm bones. They also provide support. Without them we could not stand upright. We would collapse like jelly.

The third job of bones is protection. Our brain lies inside a bony skull. The main nerve cord of the body runs down the centre of the backbone and the heart and lungs lie inside a cage of ribs.

Bones are alive. They grow and are fed by our blood with minerals and oxygen. They consist mainly of calcium and phosphorus and contain a network of fibre which gives strength. The centres of long bones are hollow with a soft marrow and a supply of blood. (*Right*) Arrows mark a greenstick fracture on an X-ray.

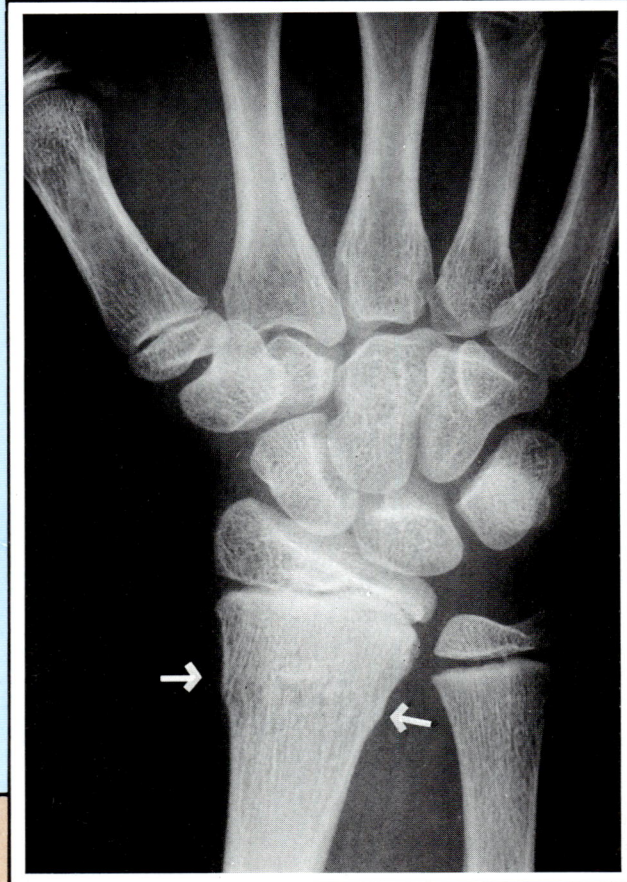

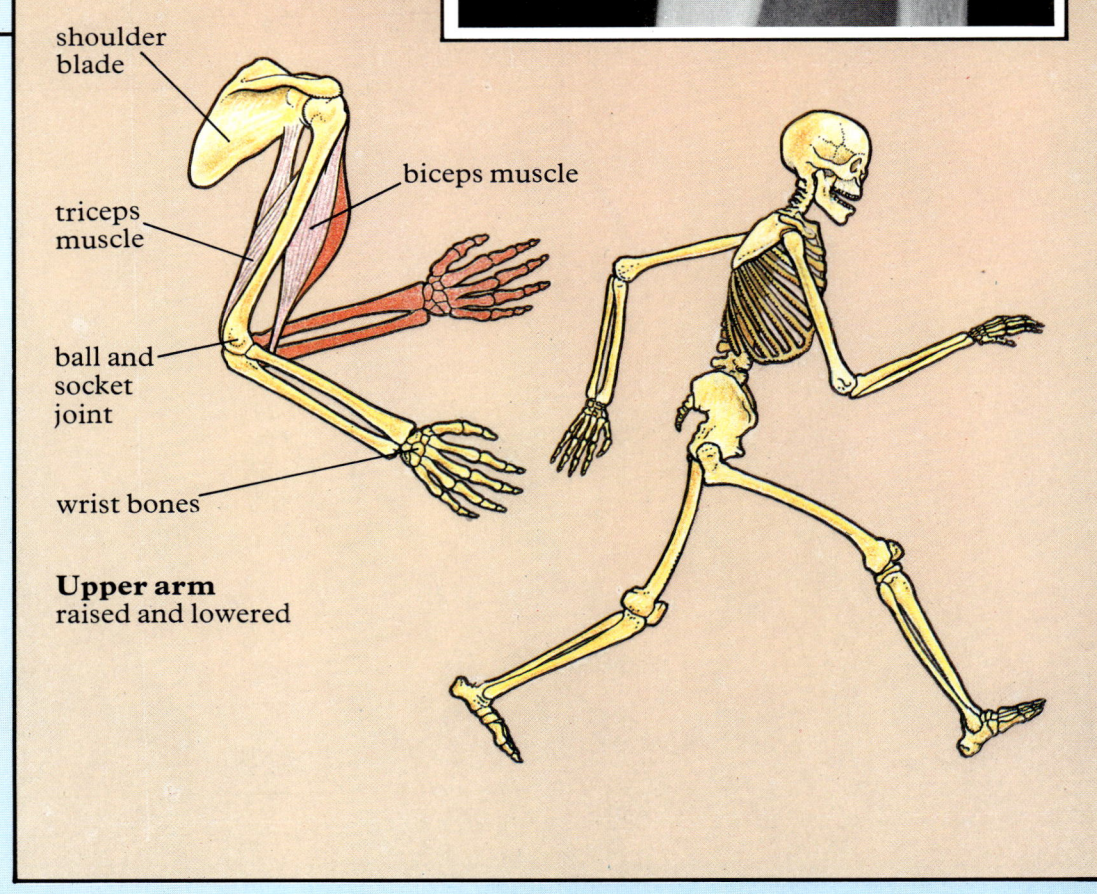

Upper arm raised and lowered

Doctors can examine our bones by using X-rays which penetrate soft flesh but show up hard bones on film. In this way they can see exactly where a bone might be broken. A bone can mend as its broken ends grow together when they are held firmly within a plaster cast.

Bones do not bend, so they must have joints to allow for movement. There are different types of joints.

The 'ball and socket' joints of the shoulders and hips allow us to rotate our arms and legs in almost any direction. But the 'hinge' joints of the knees and elbows only allow movement in one direction. Try it! A good way to illustrate a ball and socket joint is to push your right fist into the palm of your left hand. Then close that hand's fingers over the fist. Or you could look at the hitch which holds a caravan or trailer attachment to a car.

Between the elbow and the wrist there is a parallel pair of bones. The fingers, which each have four bones with hinge joints, are connected to a flexible group of small bones. These have 'sliding' joints and connect with the arm bones so the wrist can twist and bend in most directions. Ankles are similar.

At all joints the bones are held together by strong, flexible ligaments. To make movement easier the surfaces that rub against each other in the joint are covered with a smooth material called cartilage. And they are oiled with a fluid. Footballers sometimes suffer from cartilage trouble or torn ligaments.

Human teeth push through the gums when a baby is about a year old. The first set of twenty milk teeth last until they are forced out by the permanent teeth. Your teeth do different jobs. Feel your own lower teeth and you will notice that the front four are chisel-edged for cutting and biting. The next ones, on either side, are pointed for piercing and holding on to meat. Think what these teeth look like in cats or dogs. The next teeth in your mouth are small chewing teeth and the last ones, if you have them yet, are large chewing teeth.

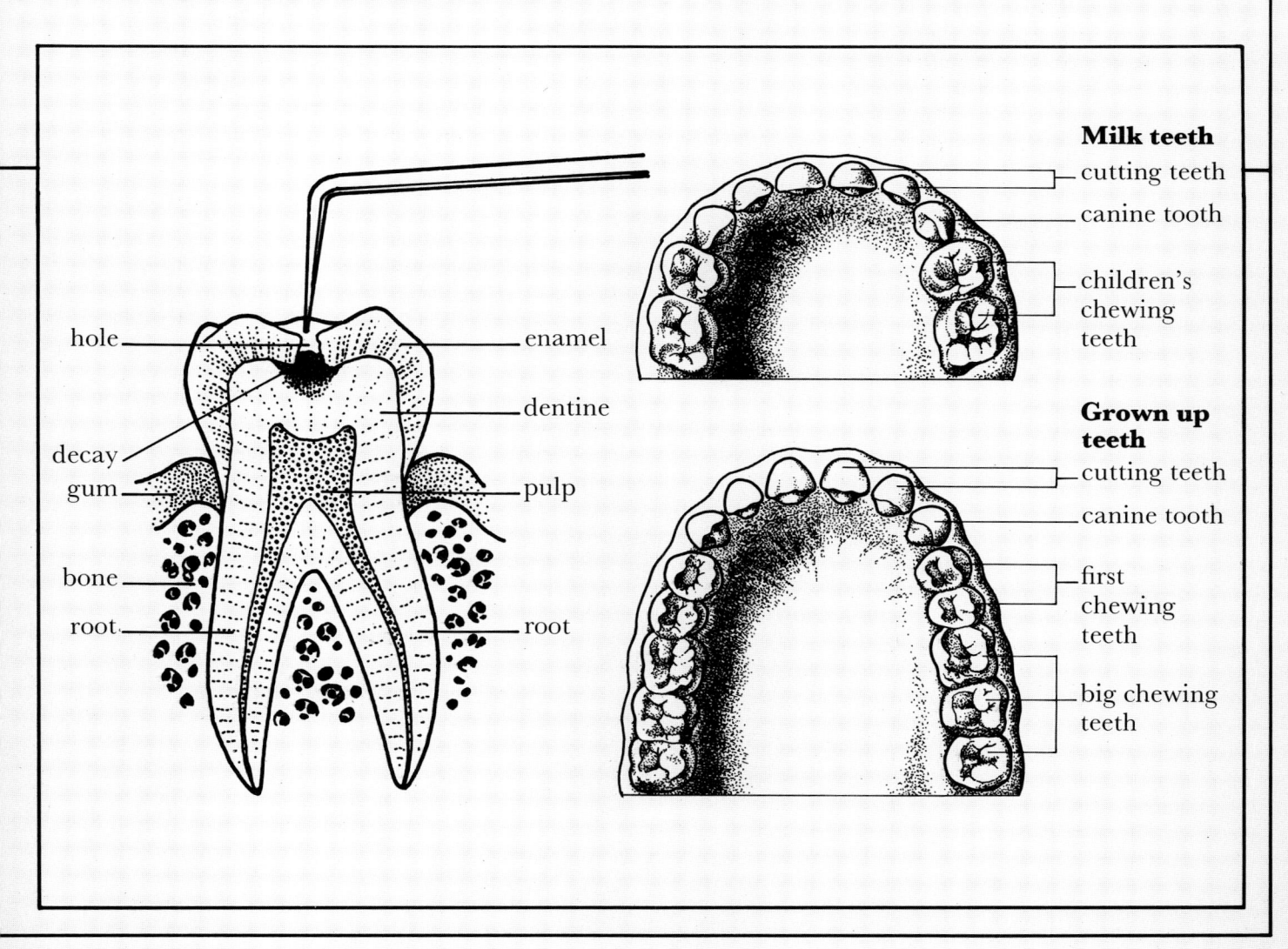

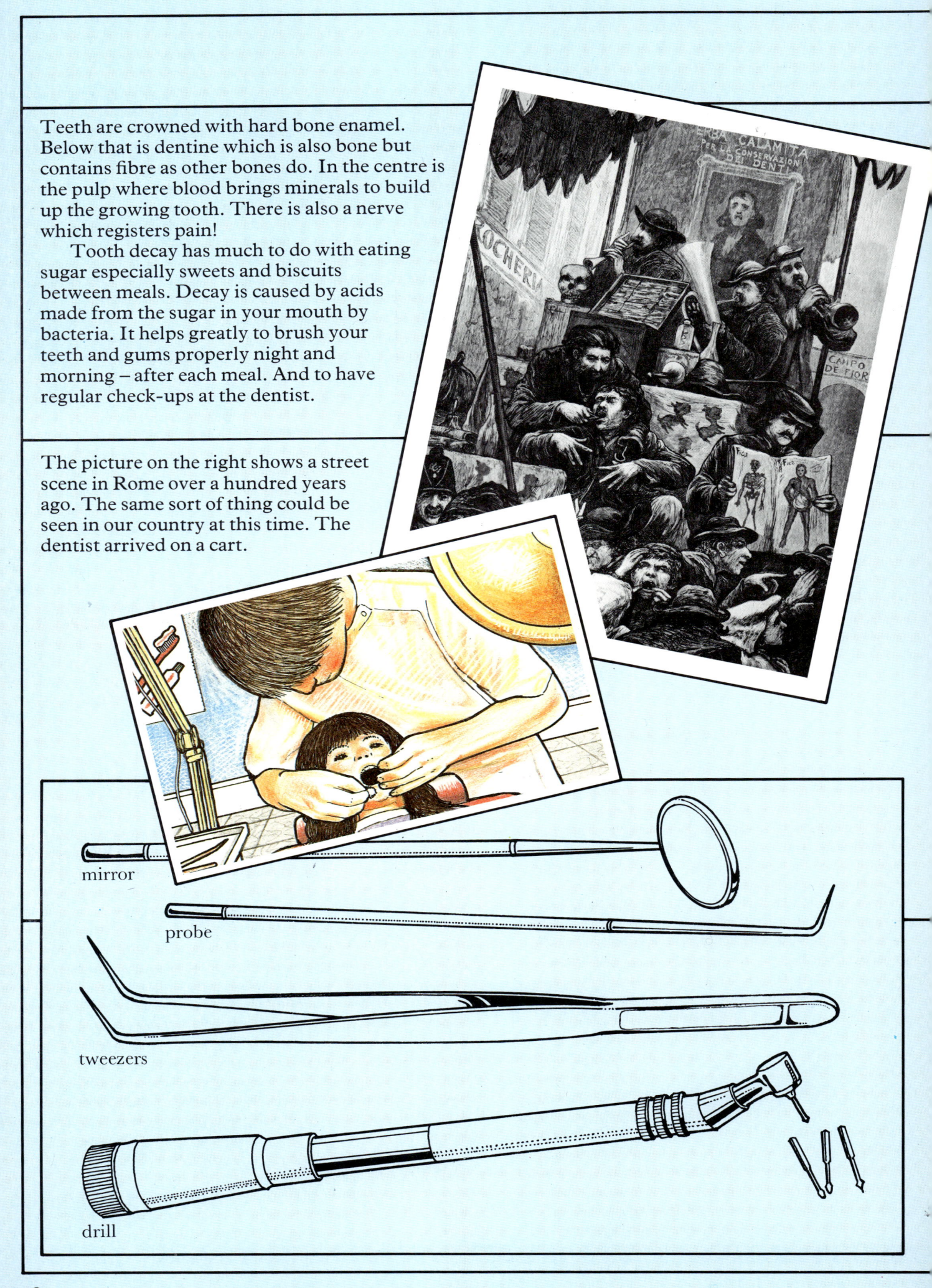

Teeth are crowned with hard bone enamel. Below that is dentine which is also bone but contains fibre as other bones do. In the centre is the pulp where blood brings minerals to build up the growing tooth. There is also a nerve which registers pain!

Tooth decay has much to do with eating sugar especially sweets and biscuits between meals. Decay is caused by acids made from the sugar in your mouth by bacteria. It helps greatly to brush your teeth and gums properly night and morning – after each meal. And to have regular check-ups at the dentist.

The picture on the right shows a street scene in Rome over a hundred years ago. The same sort of thing could be seen in our country at this time. The dentist arrived on a cart.

mirror

probe

tweezers

drill

Goldfish

Goldfish have been bred in China for thousands of years. They like an outdoor pond or a large aquarium indoors.

Fish breathe oxygen, which is dissolved in water, through their gills. Make sure that water in your aquarium or pond contains oxygenating plants like Canadian pondweed. In summer, warmer water holds less dissolved oxygen so keep your aquarium nice and fresh. If you have a pond, you may find your fish at the surface where there is most oxygen. Running water helps – a small fountain or a splashing inflow.

In winter, don't let your pond ice over. This traps poisonous gasses from decaying leaves. Do not break thick ice – the shock waves passing through the water may kill the fish. Float a ball in the water and pour a little hot water round this if the pond begins to freeze up.

Goldfish in a natural pond may find their own food, but they will need 'fish food' from May to October. In spring, the males chase the females around the pond. Eggs are released in shallow water and stick to the plants. The males then release their sperm over them and the eggs hatch to tiny 'fry' after a few days. Often the adults eat them. So try feeding extra food!

Fish kept in an indoor aquarium remain active in the winter and still need feeding. You should syphon out the water and change it regularly thus providing enough oxygen. Keep your fish out of direct light.

Frogs and tadpoles

Frogs are scarce today because there are fewer ponds to be found but frogs are specially interesting as during their lifetime they change from being water creatures to air-breathing animals on land.

Frogs hibernate in winter and become active in spring. Females lay eggs in the water and the males cast their sperms over them. The fertilised eggs float in jelly. They grow tails and after two weeks swim off to cling onto submerged plants. Gradually they develop mouths and graze on green algae. The tadpoles grow external gills to take oxygen from the water.

At four weeks, internal gills grow instead and the tadpoles begin to eat flesh – tiny pond animals or specks of meat. Tails grow longer and by seven weeks their hind legs appear.

At nine weeks, the tadpoles come to the surface and breathe air and their gills disappear. At twelve weeks, they change rapidly. Their tails are absorbed. Then their front legs appear and mouths and eyes grow larger. They become tiny frogs 2cm long. Now they must get out of the water and catch food on land.

You can help conservation by keeping only a few tadpoles, taking care to provide plant food and flesh food at the right times. Make sure that when your little frogs can climb out of the water you return them to a pond quickly.

Newts

Newts, toads and frogs are amphibians. That means that they begin life in the water rather like fish but when they are adult they can live on land and breathe air. There are three sorts of newts in Britain all with dull, green-brown colours but adult males have brightly-coloured undersides. Males of all species have crests along their backs too.

Newts have short legs, with four fingers on their front 'hands' and five toes on their hind feet. They cannot jump like frogs, but on land waddle like lizards.

When they wake up from hibernation, newts return to the water to breed. They may travel many kilometres to do this. The males shed their sperms in the water in little 'packages' and the females take them up into their bodies. This is to fertilise the eggs before they are laid. These are then deposited singly on submerged leaves. They hatch in two to four weeks and the tadpoles look more like little fish than do frog tadpoles, but they do have external gills to begin with. Later, they develop internal gills. Finally they grow lungs to breathe air.

In the autumn, newts climb out of the water and shelter in damp places until they hibernate for the winter.

Smooth newts are the commonest. Palmate newts are similar but have webbed hind feet while they are in the water. Crested newts are the largest. They may measure up to 15cm and are darker with rough, warty skins.

You can make interesting observations for your field notebook. In the spring, note the date and the stage of development of the eggs or tadpoles. Watch for adults. Which species can you see?

Pondlife

If you have a pond nearby you can observe it regularly. Draw a careful map in your field notebook and mark in where the different plants grow. Here you can see yellow flag, water mint, bistort, crowfoot and tall reedmace (bulrushes). If you have a garden, try making a pond. Design it so that frogs and newts can get in and out easily.

Moorhens visit larger ponds and smaller birds come to drink and bathe. Keep ready your binoculars, recognition book and notebook.

There will be plants below the water too – Canadian pondweed, stonewort, willow moss or broadleaved pondweeds. These oxygenate the water for the animals. There are rooted plants with floating leaves like yellow or white water lilies, or free floating plants like duckweed, or fairy moss. Crowfoot has differently shaped leaves below and on the surface. All these plants offer homes or food to a host of different animals.

A pond offers a home to many animals. To study some you need a good magnifying lens.

There are water spiders which carry down bubbles of air to their nests. And there are 'water fleas' like the Daphnia shown opposite. You can actually watch its heart beating! Keep it in a shallow dish to see this. Insect larvae include those that hatch out on the surface like the lovely damselfly, or the dragonfly with a wing span of up to 7cm.

Among carnivores is the great diving beetle which is the terror of all the smaller animals in the pond.

Caddisfly larvae live in tiny houses made by sticking little stones or pieces of stick or leaf together. A certain kind of water boatman swims on its back and pond skaters stand on the surface of the water. How many animals can you record in your field notebook?

In the pictures below you see different kinds of animal which live in and around ponds. Can you identify them?

The salmon's journey

Salmon are thought of as noble fish because of the courage and determination they show on their journey upstream.

They begin their lives in the winter when the females lay their eggs in clean gravel at the heads of streams. These hatch into 'alevins' early in the spring and after a month change into 'fry' and begin to feed on tiny animals. Yet another change takes place as they grow into 'parr'. In time they change from their mottled brown to silver and travel at springtime to the sea as 'smolt'. Here they travel widely, feeding in the shallow waters around the coasts of Britain but also as far as Greenland. After about 18 months or more some salmon return to their rivers as 'grilse'.

Adult salmon return to the river in which they spent their early lives. But how do they find their own river after months at sea and how do they know exactly when to return? They cannot see the sun or the coastline. It is a mystery. The migration up-river is known as the 'salmon run'.

Each time they enter fresh water they change their colour back again to mottled brown. They swim up-river to the identical stream where they were hatched. There they spawn a new generation. A few leave for the sea again as 'kelts' but most die as they are old and exhausted.

Salmon try to overcome any obstacle on their way up-river. They may leap up to three metres out of the water to get over a weir or waterfall. Pollution has driven the salmon out of many English rivers but in Scotland, Wales and Ireland anglers still fish for them. If you see a salmon leap that is certainly something for your notebook!

The European eel

European common eels are mysterious fish. Each year the fully-grown eels move down towards the sea. On the way, they change colour from yellow to silver. Their nostrils and eyes grow larger. In this way millions of eels migrate to the sea from the rivers of western Europe. But where do they go? None have ever been caught in the sea.

We do have a clue. For years, sailors had found great masses of transparent little 'fish', 3 to 5cm long, in the Sargasso Sea, east of the Caribbean. Some were kept in a laboratory and to everyone's surprise they grew into common eels!

Adult eels must swim to this deep part of the Atlantic Ocean to spawn and later to die. Their tiny larvae are swept back to Europe in currents.

When they reach our coasts they are about 8cm long and change into 'elvers'. Many are caught by fishermen but others swim up the rivers where they grow for some years until they are ready for the return journey. As adults, they feed on small river creatures including fish. Female eels sometimes swim across wet fields and marshes although they do not breathe air.

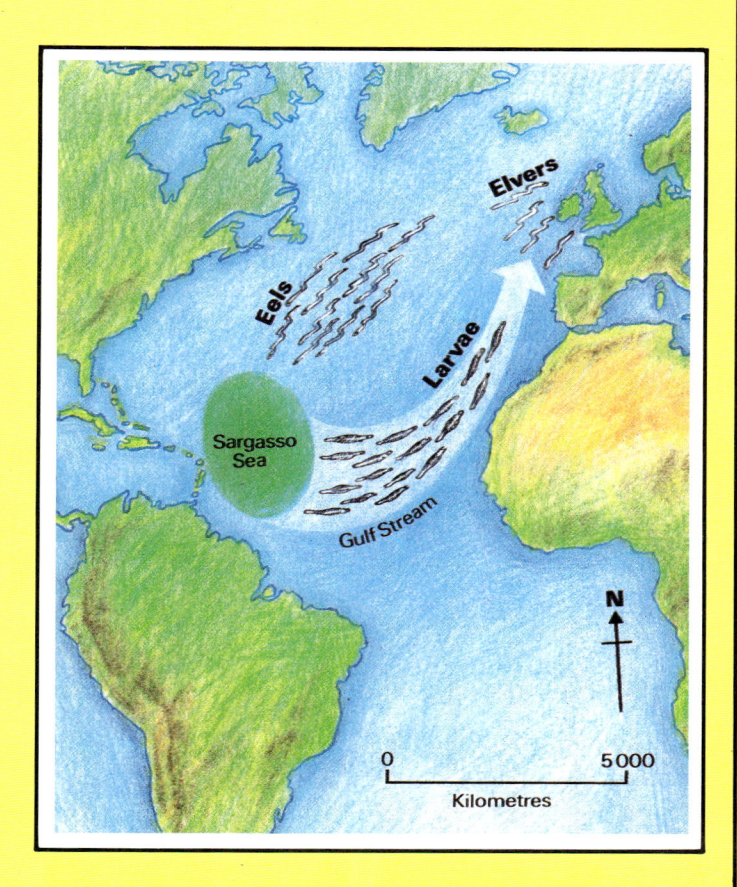

35

Flight of the swift

Swifts are adapted for long-distance flying and have been known to travel at speeds of up to a hundred kilometres an hour. In fact, apart from nesting time, they live almost entirely on the wing. Their legs are so short and weak that they only alight on the ground by accident. And if they do, they have difficulty in taking off again! They even sleep and mate on the wing.

Swifts swoop and turn to catch flies, moths or flying beetles in their gaping mouths. You may think that they look black but actually they are a very dark brown with a pale chin patch. Their wings are very long, curved and pointed. And their tails are short and forked. For fast flying their shape could not be improved!

Each year they arrive in Britain in late April or early May. They nearly always return to the same nesting site and their untidy nests are made of feathers, straw and their own saliva. They are built in roofs, towers, or in crevices on cliffs. Swifts nest close together in colonies but each pair defends its own patch fiercely.

Two or three white eggs are laid and the young hatch after three weeks' incubation by the parents. Both parents then feed them until they are about six weeks old.

Sometimes on fine days the whole swift colony flies round its area screaming with high-pitched cries.

In early July, young swifts take the plunge and fly. Once they are airborne there is no going back! So they must chase their own food, although their parents may continue for a time to feed them as well. They need to build up their strength for the long journey to Africa.

Swifts leave in groups, adults first, in August or September. For most of the journey they fly at a height of more than one thousand metres and it takes them about thirty days.

The most difficult parts of the flight will be crossing the Alps or Pyrenees mountains in Europe, and the Sahara desert in Africa. That is about one thousand kilometres wide. They also have to fly over hot jungles to reach their feeding areas in Central Africa.

Here they stay until April next year when they begin their flight to Europe. How they find their way is a mystery. Young swifts migrate without any help from their parents. It is thought that they navigate by the position of the sun and stars.

A naturalist always notes down the dates when he first sees bird visitors of summer and the dates when they leave. If you observe a swifts' nesting colony you can note down its exact location. Then you will be able to come to the same place next year and see them again. You may be able to save a young swift if it falls from its nest and cannot get off the ground. Place it in as high a place as you can. The parents may come and feed it and, after a rest, it may be able to fly.

Warblers

If the migration of swallows is extraordinary, what about these little birds? Every year they make the same journey to and from northern Africa or southern Europe.

It is not easy to tell one warbler from another. The tiny chiff-chaff (*below left*) is only 11cm long. It is our first summer visitor to arrive towards the end of March. You may not see chiff-chaffs easily but you will certainly hear their distinctive calls from the tops of trees in woods or parks. Each male quickly takes up a territory. Here the females builds a nest of grass and leaves not in the tree tops but low in the undergrowth.

Chiff-chaffs give you a good opportunity to map territories in your field notebook. Walk slowly through a wood and listen. Each chiff-chaff will be singing in his own patch but as you move to his neighbour's he will retreat. So you can mark the boundaries of each territory.

Willow warblers (*below*) look like chiff-chaffs even to experts. But the song is quite different. It is really a warbling song of rippling notes. These birds arrive in April from further south in Africa. Whitethroats make for a hedge or open common. Because of droughts in parts of Africa fewer arrive today.

Certain people have special permission to catch and ring birds (in the picture a lesser whitethroat). The ring bears its own number and the address of the British Museum in London. Anyone finding the bird in another country can return the ring to the museum. This is how we discover the routes and flying distances of migrating birds.

Worldwide conservation

A message from Cyril Littlewood MBE, Director of Young People's Trust for Endangered Species (YPTES).

All over the world the wealth of animal and plant life is fast disappearing. Quite a number of these animals and plants survive in such small populations that they are probably beyond help and may soon disappear for ever.

It is hardly surprising that there are so many endangered species. Take, for instance, the mountain gorillas of central Africa. Their jungle forests are being cut down to make way for farmland. And all over the world humans are taking more and more land for housing, farming, factories, shops, offices, schools, hospitals, roads and airports. The wild land is being gobbled up at an alarming speed.

We are still killing some great whales even though we know that we may wipe out all the existing species within just a few years of this book being published. Until very recently (*see bottom picture*) whaling was not controlled at all.

National parks and nature reserves can be established or extended so that animal and plant species can be protected.

Endangered species can, to some extent, be bred in captivity.

Strict laws are needed worldwide so that wild animals and plants can be protected. We also need to protect their habitats – their living places.

Trade in wildlife products such as furs for coats must be strictly controlled everywhere.

Most of all, we need people – and especially *young people* – to be willing to learn more about our world and how to care for that wealth of wildlife in the future.

Observing and painting animals

In zoos we can see animals from all over the world. A good naturalist will want to do more than just rush around looking at everything.

It is worthwhile spending time observing some animals closely and drawing careful sketches for your field notebook. Later, you can colour them as our artist, Maurice Wilson, has painted these pictures.

See how he has captured not just the shapes and markings but also the feelings of the animals.
Each picture tells a story.
The alert kudu grazing on the African plains is aware of its predator – the lion! It is one of the biggest kinds of antelope and is beautifully marked. Just the animal to tempt an artist.

The chimpanzee is curling his lip – a sign of fear. And as for the Rhesus monkeys – you can almost hear the father sternly scolding his children! The artist has spent a long time watching and getting the details right.

You may not be as gifted as Maurice Wilson but remember that he had to work hard to develop his skill. You will improve if you keep trying and your field notebook will have a further interest for you!

Bengal tiger

Tigers are big cats. They are ruthless hunters and are kings of the jungle in Asia!

Tigers are wonderfully camouflaged and hunt by stalking their prey through long grass rather than by running in the open. Maurice Wilson's picture shows the tiger's strong, muscular body and conveys its great strength.

Deer, goats and cattle are taken by tigers but occasionally they have raided villages and killed human beings. Country people in Asia greatly fear them. Many years ago, European big-game hunters and Indian princes organised hunts for tigers with hundreds of beaters. Very many tigers were shot. In our time, the Indian government has set up a special reserve for them. Tigers need huge areas to hunt in and it was not easy to spare the land. But now the last wild tigers are protected.

Wolves

'Who's afraid of the big bad wolf?' Wolves are often the villains of our stories – like the wolf in Red Riding Hood. On the other hand, Red Indians admired wolves and called them their brothers.

Wolves are carnivores and hunt their prey. It is thought that about twenty thousand years ago men domesticated some wolves and from these came our breeds of dogs. Today, wild wolves are found in Russia, northern Canada and Alaska, but rarely in Europe.

Wolves mate in January or February and the cubs are born in April or May. The female prepares two dens which are holes in the ground under trees or rocks. Her cubs are born in the first and about a week later she transfers them to the second den about 200 metres away. Other females may help to feed the young as they grow.

Wolves are strong animals and are about as big as Alsatian dogs. They can travel 40 kilometres in a day but each wolf pack has its territory and outsiders will be driven off. Hunting in packs means that wolves have to work together and communicate with each other in a number of ways. They do not bark but howl and this is thought to be for the purpose of telling others where they are. By urinating on trees or rocks, or rubbing these with their scent glands, wolves mark out their territories. In each pack there is a strict order of importance from the leader to the humblest member. Only if the pack is broken up and the order disturbed will wolves fight each other.

Their natural prey is the large herds of caribou in Canada or reindeer in northern Europe. But wolves will eat any small animal they can find. With their strong canine teeth they can tear and swallow meat very quickly. But they can then go many days without food.

You may never see wolves in the wild. The last one in Britain was killed in Scotland about two hundred years ago.

Kangaroos

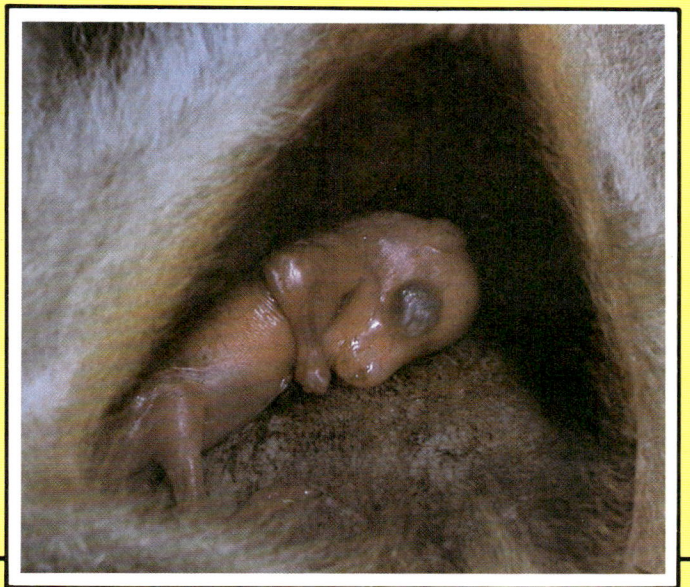

Kangaroos, like many other Australian animals, are marsupials. And like other marsupials they have small brains and the females carry their young in pouches. Inside the pouch the baby 'joey' can feed on milk but in the picture you see a mother grey kangaroo with a baby perfectly able to feed on grass. He hops out to feed and jumps back in for comfort and safety!

In another picture, you see a baby kangaroo just after it has been born. It measures 3 or 4cm so it is only very tiny at birth and has to tunnel through its mother's fur to find her pouch.

Kangaroos include many different types as well as the large grey ones over 2 metres tall. They mostly have short front paws and powerful hind legs. Their heavy tails can be used for balancing when they hop. Hopping is their way of moving fast. A grey kangaroo can leap a distance of 12 metres and a height of 2.5 metres.

Grey and red kangaroos live in the open plains. Wallabies are smaller and prefer scrubland with bushes and rocks. Some are a metre long with tails measuring another metre but others are as small as rabbits! 'Kangaroo rats' are the smallest type of kangaroo and measure less than 40cm long.

Today, in Australia, kangaroos and wallabies are in urgent need of protection. Efforts are now being made to conserve them yet some are still hunted for their skins and meat. Many farmers want to get rid of kangaroos as they eat grass put down for sheep and cattle. They are also persecuted by the 'wild dog' of Australia, the dingo. It is thought that this dog came over with native people a long time ago. These Aboriginal people settled in Australia and many of their dogs went wild.

Marsupials are strange animals which are not able to live successfully alongside other kinds of mammals. In the great island of Australia they had the land to themselves for a long time and multiplied. But unfortunately man has introduced other mammals and the 'wild dog' is only one of these. Rats and rabbits came with the early settlers and marsupials were not good at facing competition. Many kinds died out altogether.

Since Australia was settled by Europeans about two hundred years ago life has become more and more difficult for the marsupials, including the kangaroos.

American bison

Bison, or buffaloes, are 'cattle'. They have cloven hooves, eat grass (herbivores) and chew the cud (ruminants).

American buffaloes may weigh up to 1 tonne. Before Europeans came to America in large numbers, say about the year 1800, there were fifty million buffaloes. Their grazing kept the prairie grass cropped. The story of what happened is a grim lesson as these magnificent animals might have been lost for ever. By 1810 there were none east of the Mississippi but about twenty million buffaloes remained on the great western plains. Originally they were hunted by Red Indians on foot, providing meat, skins and bones for tools. Europeans introduced the horse to America. Soon after came other Europeans with guns. They killed over a million buffaloes in just one year to make room for their longhorn cattle and sheep. By 1872 only seven million were left and by 1882 they were hunting the last herd of ten thousand animals. In 1897 the last four in Colorado were killed.

A protected herd survived in Canada and there were a few buffaloes in zoos. But a Red Indian conservationist named Walking Coyote captured four calves in 1873 and his herd grew to seven hundred animals by 1906. In 1905, conservationists collected forty buffaloes and started a protected herd in Montana. Now there are twenty thousand buffaloes in the USA.

There are other kinds of buffaloes in Asia and, very rarely, in Europe.

Camels

We think of camels living in the hot deserts of Arabia and the Sahara. These are Arabian one-humped camels (*picture below*). They have been domesticated for thousands of years. Today, trucks provide transport but camels are still cheap and can carry 150 kilos. They feed on rough shrubs and can last a few days without water. Their humps contain reserves of fat.

Arabian camels have large padded feet for walking in soft sand. They can close their nostrils against sandstorms. Camels also provide meat, milk, hair and skins. Rich Arabs have racing camels.

The domesticated Bactrian camels of Northern China (*top right*) have two humps for added reserves when there is little food. They have thick coats and the pads on their feet are hard which helps them to survive in cold rocky deserts.

There is another group of animals, similar to camels. These are the llamas of South America. They have no humps and more hair. Some are still wild.

How do these groups come to be spread so widely? Fossil evidence shows that camels first lived in North America. Some migrated across a land bridge to Asia, others to South America.

You may only see camels in zoos. Compare their similar heads and feet.

Wildlife in the city

Wildlife in the city? That does not seem to be quite right does it? Yet wherever there is an empty plot of land a plant will grow! Waste land, where buildings have been knocked down, can support many wild plants. Ivy, moss and lichens grow on the walls and on high ledges elder, or long branches of buddleia may be seen. Rosebay willowherb is the most striking plant to grow on these sites and its tall pink flowers are seen everywhere. Coltsfoot with its grey leaves and yellow flowers is also one of the first to arrive when a site is cleared. But others quickly follow. Yellow ragwort is found among old bricks and wild parsley grows on exposed soil.

The seeds of some of these wild plants are spread by wind. Ragwort is thought to have travelled by rail! Its seeds can be carried in the slip-stream of express trains. You might like to examine wind-borne seeds to see how they float on tiny parachutes of fluff. Elder seeds are carried by birds which eat the berries and pass out the undigested seeds with their droppings. Other seeds are spread by human shoes or the wheels of vehicles which have run over mud elsewhere. Butterbur seeds with little hooks are carried by animals on their fur or by humans on trouser legs! How many different wild flowers can you see in the illustrations or find for yourself on a waste site?

Once plants have arrived at a site animals will follow. Indeed, some may get there first. Lift carefully a piece of corrugated iron or paving stone that has lain on the ground for some time and you may see beneath it the home of a woodlouse (*below*), tunnelling beetles, ants, worms or perhaps a mouse's nest! Grasshoppers may be heard on sunny banks and spiders will be everywhere. If the site is within reach of a park you may also find hedgehogs. The handsome Roman snail in the picture grazes on the soft plant tissue of grass too. Sometimes grass snakes curl up among the debris. And you might find toads hiding in dark damp places!

Of course bumble-bees may nest in walls and visit the flowers. Watch out for signs of rats – there are bound to be some around. Birds will look in, too, such as town pigeons and starlings seeking any scraps they can find. And blue tits and great tits eat the seeds of any shrubs. Their enemies, kestrels for instance, hunt for mice or small birds. And owls may hunt by night. There are likely to be feral cats which are domestic cats which have gone 'wild'. Many foxes now hunt through cities at night and hide away in the daytime. Do not forget there are parks and gardens too. These can be excellent living places for wildlife.

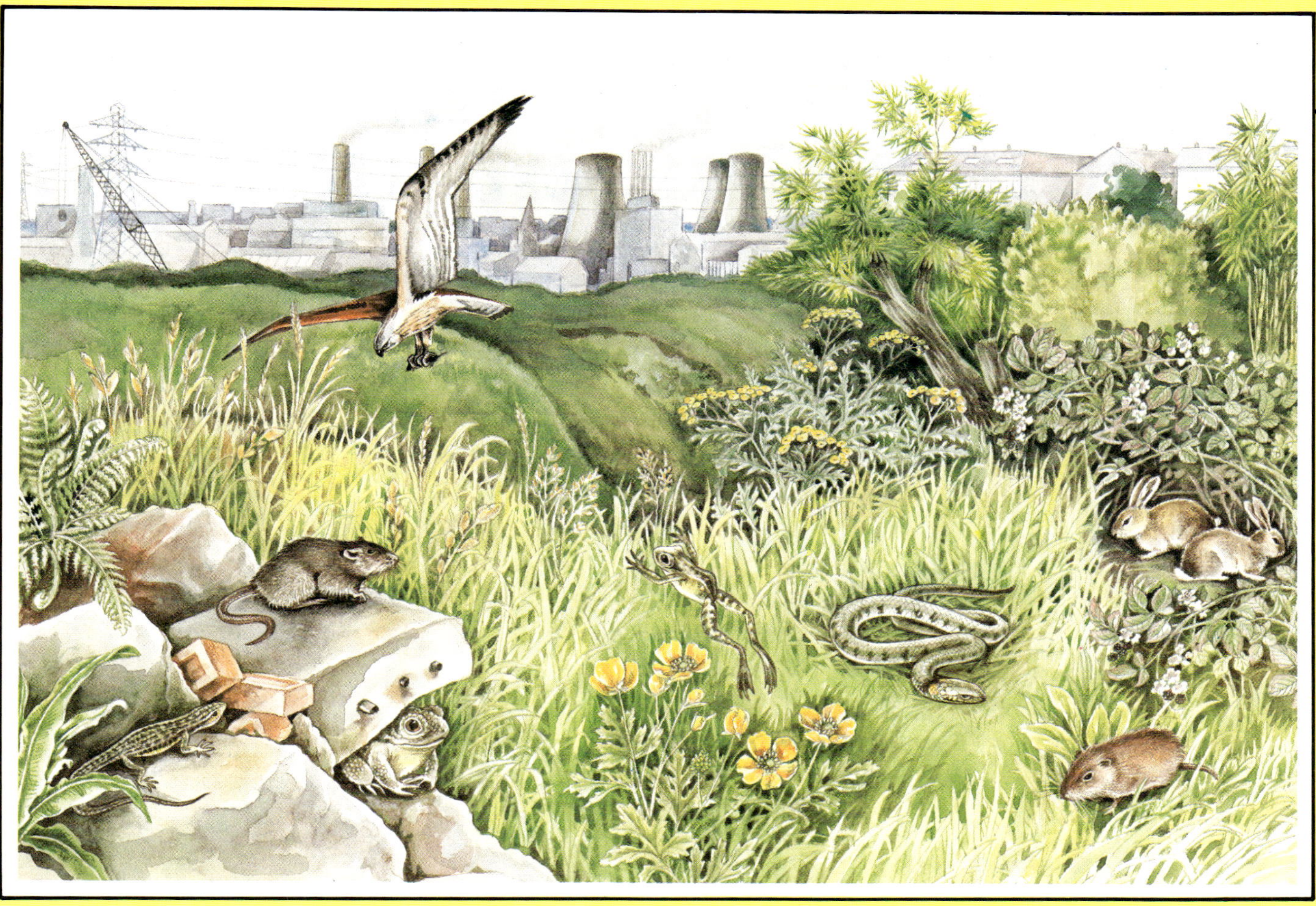

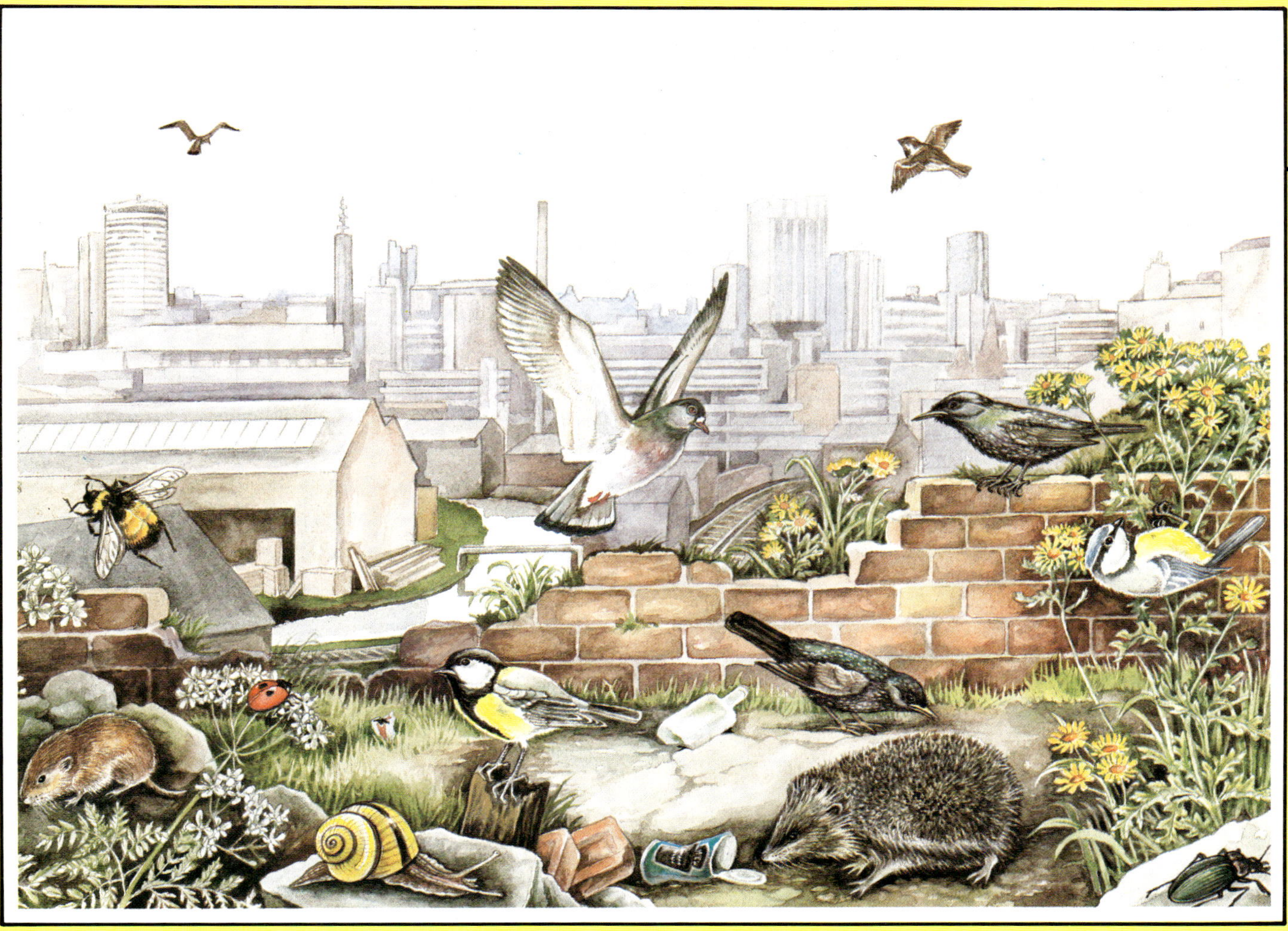

Springtime

Spring begins officially on 21 March. By that date daylight and darkness are of equal length. From then on, the daylight gets longer each day. The extra sunlight warms up the soil and this in turn warms the air. Seeds need warmth and moisture so that they can germinate. The leaves of green plants need the energy of sunlight to make the plants' food. Every Spring plants that have been dormant or 'sleeping' in the winter begin to grow again. Their buds push out into new leaves.

Animals like hedgehogs awake from their hibernation. Others like squirrels that have just been sheltering from the cold come out to feed. Visiting birds arrive from the south, and resident birds establish their territories. Then they begin to mate and breed. Winter visitors on the other hand fly off to breeding lands in the far north.

Below, you see a pair of ravens. These are birds of mountain and rocky sea coasts and are found in northern and western parts of Britain. They are members of the crow family and are early nesters. Many young ravens will be flying by Easter.

Spring is an exciting time to use your field notebook. Here are some things to look out for.

Note the dates you hear the first chiff-chaff or if you are lucky, the first cuckoo. Or when you see the first swallows.

Watch for the first spring flowers in your garden, in the park, in hedgerows or on waste ground. Try to recognise them from a wild flower book. Do not pick them of course – take the book to the flowers, never the other way round. Draw them or photograph them. Make careful observations. What colour are they? How many petals do they have? Draw the outline of the shape of the leaf. Measure the height of the plant. Then look it up. You will quickly learn to recognise dandelions, coltsfoot, buttercups, daisies and others. On the right you can see spring primroses.

Animals are found everywhere in spring. Worms come out when the soil has thawed. Snails or slugs move along their glistening trails. Hibernating butterflies re-appear.

49

Even to people who live in cities, spring has a special feeling. After the cold winter comes warmer sunshine and the daylight lengthens. Heating is turned down and folk can go out into the park, the streets or their gardens. Spring is even more dramatic in the countryside. No longer does everyone wake up to see white frosts over the fields. Hedges and trees have green leaf-buds or blossom. The first green shoots push up out of the earth.

Catkins are a sign of spring. The pussy willows in the picture are the male flowers of the willow. Some willow trees are male, others are female. Hazel catkins, called 'lambs' tails' are also male flowers. But if you look carefully you will find tiny, red female flowers on the same branches. Look on oak or poplar trees to find other catkins.

Blackthorn or sloe blossom (*see below*) comes out before its leaves. It is one of the loveliest sights of spring. Sloe used to be grown in countryside hedgerows but over the last two hundred years hawthorn has been more popular. If you examine the flowers you will see that they have the same structure as all the wild members of the rose family. They are arranged in fives – petals, stamens for pollen and ovaries for seeds.

Unlike catkins, these flowers have male and female parts within the same flower.

Pale blue forget-me-nots (*see below*) are from another family. Generally, they flower in their second spring. Different kinds of forget-me-not grow in woodland and in wet places.

Adders and grass snakes

Snakes make unusual entries in your field notebook! Watch carefully for them but never try to touch them. As they are reptiles they cannot control their body temperature. That means that they warm up in the sun and slow down in the cold. So in winter, in this country, they have to hibernate. Unlike lizards they have no eyelids or outer ears. They lay eggs with soft, leathery shells. Sometimes the females keep the eggs inside their bodies until they are almost ready to hatch. If snakes are frightened they may put out a smelly fluid in defence. Their forked tongues are for smelling and sensing and slip through a special notch when the mouth is closed. The upper jaws are hinged so that they can swallow large prey.

Grass snakes, sometimes called ringed snakes, vary in colour. Mostly, they are olive-green or brown with black spots on their scaly bodies. They are found only in England and Wales in woodlands, hedges and marshes where they can even climb trees and swim. Frogs, newts and tadpoles are their favourite food. Their bites are not poisonous. Sometimes they pretend to be dead, as in the picture, and this is a good form of defence. Grass snakes mate in April or May and about six weeks later thirty or so eggs are laid in a warm place such as a manure heap (see picture, bottom right).

Two months later, the young crawl out, fending for themselves at once. They measure about 17cm and grow to about a metre in adulthood. Adders, or vipers, are found all over Britain except Ireland. They may be seen in places which catch the sun. You will recognise the zig-zag pattern along their backs but as they are very alert they are hard to surprise. Small animals like frogs and birds are their main food. They kill them with poison which passes down a pair of hollow fangs. (Below) Adder with young.

Adders mate in spring too, but the young are born as little snakes from eggs held in the females' bodies, in August or September. Adders are naturally timid. Their poison, though dangerous to children, hardly ever kills adults.

Slow worms and lizards

Lizards are land reptiles. They cannot control their body temperatures so they grow cold and hibernate for the winter. They have scales and shed their skins a number of times as they grow.

Some lizards appear to be born not as eggs but as miniature adults. When they emerge from the female they are surrounded by a thin shell and break out of it straight away. To do this they have special egg teeth and it happens both in common lizards and slow worms.

The common lizard is found all over Britain and parts of Ireland. In fact, it is the only reptile native to Ireland. Colour varies from brown to green or grey. Walls or hedges, woods, sand dunes, even mountains or boggy places provide its home. It is a good climber and can run up a smooth wall easily. The common lizard eats insects and larvae, but especially spiders. In early summer it will mate and the young are born in late summer or autumn. Although they come out of thin-skinned eggs they are well-developed and the mother hides them.

Slow worms are completely harmless, legless lizards. They are found all over Britain but not in Ireland. Adults may be 25cm long. At dusk they feed on spiders, slugs and similar small animals. They mate in early summer and are born in autumn in thin-skinned eggs. Slow worms have many enemies and other lizards eat them. So do hedgehogs, snakes or large birds. From October they begin their winter hibernation under piles of leaves.

Sand lizards are not common. Their homes are in sandy places, especially dunes, mainly in the south of England. Colour and markings vary but they are usually greenish, especially the males. They like to dig burrows in the sand and eat spiders and all kinds of insects, although they dislike hairy caterpillars. Mating is in early summer and eggs are laid in shallow holes, in June or July, in batches of around a dozen. They are soft-shelled and pink. After seven to twelve weeks, according to the temperature, they hatch.

Right Male and female sand lizards

Below left Male common lizard

Below right Male, female and young slow worms

Pollution problems

In the pictures, below, you see some of the results of man's influence upon his world. High stack chimneys belch forth waste and poisonous gases into the atmosphere. These gases may be manufactured by factories or power stations. But most of the poison that we put into the air comes from the exhaust gases of vehicles such as cars and lorries.

British cities used to be choked with fumes and soot from the burning of coal. Sometimes, especially in winter, it was nearly impossible to see more than a few metres ahead. This was in the days of smog and you might like to ask an adult about it.

Nowadays, we are more able to control the amount of waste gases we put out. Our cities are cleaner than they used to be and the air is purer for breathing. Buildings do not become so quickly marked with dirt.

However, there is much still to be done to make our air truly pure. Some poisonous gases, such as sulphur dioxide, oxides of nitrogen and carbon monoxide cannot be seen and we still push them out into the air. Sometimes we pretend that our problems have blown away in the wind! But sulphur dioxide, produced by our power stations, may be carried across the North Sea and affect other countries. It makes an acid with rain water. Rain falling in these countries can be fairly acid and when it collects in lakes it can kill off many living creatures including fish.

In the other picture, you can see a sea-going vessel putting out oil and ploughing its way through an oil slick. Even though there are International Laws aimed at preventing ships from doing this very large amounts of oil continue to pass into our oceans.

Certain seabirds such as guillemots and razorbills often rest on the surface of the sea. They can be engulfed by an oil spillage and choke to death as a result. Sometimes they are washed up on our beaches; people try to rescue them but very few survive. Their warm coating of feathers is ruined by the oil. This means that their body heat escapes and they die from cold and exhaustion.

Have you sat on a beach, on holiday, and then noticed blobs of thick, tarry oil nearby? On many of our beaches it is all too easy to pick up staining oil on our feet or shoes or clothing.

Yet it is easy to criticise people who cause pollution and ruin the world. Most of us would agree that we need cars, aeroplanes, ships, oil, houses, roads and factories which make things. Yet cannot all this be done so that we do not wreck our beautiful world at the same time? It is not an easy problem to solve.

Hedgerows and roadsides

Hedges were planted for a purpose – to keep cattle and sheep in and to keep raiders out! Now farming methods have changed and hedges are disappearing from the countryside. Farmers today use giant machines which work best in bigger fields where cereal crops are planted. Far fewer animals are kept in fields and in some counties hedges are being taken out altogether. The practice of burning off waste straw, or stubble, after the corn harvest sometimes results in burning out the hedges too.

A few thousand years ago the early settlers left strips of woodland between their fields. Gradually these narrowed into boundary hedges. Other hedges were planted by the Normans nearly one thousand years ago. And more hedges have been planted since those times. Over the last two hundred years common fields have been enclosed by hedge boundaries.

In the southern half of Britain you can make a fair guess at the age of a hedge. Count the number of different kinds of woody shrubs or trees in a 30 metre length. This will give the *approximate* age in centuries. One kind for each hundred years.

An 'enclosure' hedge planted in the last century may still consist entirely of hawthorn. The rule above cannot be applied in the north and west where hedges grow differently and stone walls are common.

Old hedges and road verges are the homes of many woodland plants and animals as well as old meadow flowers such as the poppies shown here. Yellowhammers, as in the picture, often nest in old hedges. Meadow brown butterflies and many other butterflies find their food plants there. Councils responsible for looking after roadside verges should take care not to cut them when these plants are flowering. Conservationists ask councils not to spray roadside verges with chemicals which kill the wild plants or insects on which so many other animals depend for food. You may have seen machines cutting wild grasses and flowers when they are in bloom.

You will quickly recognise the important hedge plants. The most common is hawthorn which is strong, thorny and grows quickly. You will also find blackthorn.

Hazel and field maple have no thorns but their supple branches can be woven across gaps. Trees grow in hedges and ash, oak and elm are the most often seen. Their timber used to be useful to farmers when they had to make their own implements and carts.

Old hedgerows and verges support a host of wild flowers. In spring, primroses, celandines and wild arums grow in shady places especially if there is a ditch by the hedge. White stitchwort grows up among the grass and the stiff stems of hedge parsley can be seen everywhere. You may even find giant hogweeds or cow parsley growing a couple of metres tall! In summer, many other plants appear such as thistles and knapweeds and white and red campions, dandelions and plants of the same family like hawkweeds and daisies. You might also find clover and many sorts of nettles with white, yellow or red flowers as well as the familiar stinging nettles. In some areas you may find ferns or bracken. Wild grasses are worth looking at. When their heads are grown you can distinguish more than a dozen different kinds quite easily. You will also find wild cherries, wild pears, crab apples and evergreen holly. Blackberries, brambles and the pink dog roses, shown in the picture, climb among the stronger shrubs.

In autumn, you will be cheered by the beautiful colours of maple and cherry leaves. The fruits attract many birds fattening themselves up before the winter. Besides the red haws and black sloes there will be red and yellow crab apples, brown acorns and the brilliant scarlet berries of bryony. There may be an elder bush with bunches of juicy black fruits. Blackberries, elderberries and sloes are still used by country people for jam and wine-making.

Living among the flowers are insects and other small animals. There are also butterflies and moths to identify. You could list the snails, grasshoppers, aphids, ladybirds, dragonflies, beetles and the many other creatures which make their homes in a hedge. There are insect eaters such as spiders, frogs, toads and the small mammals. Woodmice, as in the picture, nest at the bottom of the hedge. But hunters such as weasels on the ground or kestrels in the air are always watching. Many birds nest in hedges like the wren, in the picture, which creeps through the undergrowth. Robins and blackbirds may nest higher up.

Hedges and roadside verges are full of activity from spring to autumn so keep your notebook and hand lens near you.

Beetles

Beetles have hard wing cases that close together covering over a second pair of wings. They are insects with antennae and have jaws for biting. In Britain, there are some four thousand different kinds so you are not likely ever to see them all!

The picture (*below*) shows stag beetles which live in woods in southern England. The males, which are 7.5cm long, are the biggest beetles in Britain. Their 'antlers' are really jaws.

Great diving beetles have a very different habitat. They live in ponds or streams and come up to fetch a supply of air about every ten minutes. Any small animals in the water are their prey. Females lay their eggs on water plants. The larvae, which hatch from the eggs, are fierce hunters and eat tadpoles! These beetles, like stag beetles, need to be protected in their proper habitats. Like some other insects they have been collected on such a scale that they are becoming scarce.

The third beetles shown are burying beetles so called because they bury small animals such as dead birds or mice found on the woodland floor. Usually a group of beetles works together. The female lays her eggs nearby. When the larvae emerge the parents feed them on the decaying carcass until they can manage for themselves. After a few months clean bones are all that is left!

There are many other beetles which you will be able to note. Among the most common are ladybirds, two-spotted or seven-spotted. Their larvae feed on aphids such as greenfly.

Ground beetles are found everywhere under stones and come out at night to hunt small animals. Bark beetles attack trees and spread Dutch Elm disease. And furniture beetles attack wooden furniture in homes. Their larvae leave little holes once they have eaten their way through.

Death-watch beetles often live in old timbers in church roofs where their larvae tunnel out the wood. The adults make a tapping sound and this is how they got their name. They were heard when people watched over a coffin through the night.

Grasshoppers and crickets

In Britain, there are fifteen different kinds of crickets and six kinds of grasshoppers and they are hard to tell apart. They each have four wings and an especially long pair of legs for jumping. In fact, once you know what to do, you can spot the differences. Crickets have long feelers and grasshoppers have short ones. The crickets make their whirring sounds by rubbing together rough edges on their fore-wings. Grasshoppers sing by rubbing their wings with their long legs. Both types have strange 'ears' on their legs and possess large eyes consisting of thousands of tiny lenses. As they are insects they have an interesting life-cycle. But there is no 'maggot' stage. The nymphs which emerge from the eggs look just like tiny adults and cast their skins as they grow.

Some crickets and grasshoppers eat only grass. Others may eat insects. The female crickets have long pointed egg-tubes which are used to pierce the soil. They have a hollow tube inside and eggs are forced down this and laid under the surface.

The largest crickets you may find in Britain are the great green bush crickets and measure up to 5cm long. You can see one in the picture. They actually walk rather than hop, but if you startle them they can jump or even glide short distances. As they are carnivorous they eat smaller insects. On road verges or in old meadows, crickets can often be heard whirring in the sunshine for long periods by rubbing their forewings together. You could try to find them and if you are very careful, you can keep them in view to make a quick sketch for your field notebook.

Field grasshoppers (*left*) are smaller than crickets and have short antennae. They are relatives of the locusts of Africa but cause no danger in our country!

Black field crickets, measuring about 3cm long, are shown here but are uncommon. They are not often seen because they live mainly below the soil in tunnels. House crickets used to live in warm places in houses and came out to feed at night. Once they were very common and as 'the cricket on the hearth' their whirring noises were quite popular. Vacuum cleaners have put an end to the dust and crumbs they lived on so they are not often found today.

Caterpillars and butterflies

Butterflies urgently need our protection so it is best not to collect them. Instead we can watch, admire and record them whenever we can. And we may come across a rare one!

There are about sixty kinds of butterfly in Britain of which only about thirty are widespread. Each sort needs its own special food plant and butterfly habitats are being destroyed by modern farming. Some may disappear altogether from our countryside.

The picture shows the life-story of the small tortoiseshell butterfly. Adults emerge from hibernation in early spring. In May, they lay their eggs on the undersides of young nettle leaves. When they hatch the young caterpillars spin a silky covering round themselves for protection. As they grow they cast their skins a number of times and in June they pupate. This means that they undergo a mysterious change from slow, crawling caterpillars to beautiful, flying butterflies. Before pupation the caterpillars find hiding places where they hang from threads. Their skins harden into brown cases. In July, the first new butterflies emerge from the pupae and hang upside down to dry their soft wings. Quickly they fly off to mate and the female later produces further broods.

As caterpillars they hardly ever stop eating plant material but when they become butterflies they only sip nectar from flowers with their long curled tongues.

Remember that you can help butterflies by providing the right kind of flowers and wild plants for their caterpillars.

Bumblebees

If you can find a bumble-bee nest you will find it fascinating to watch. Generally these are in crevices in walls or trees, or sometimes in long uncut grass. There are sixteen different sorts of bumble-bee in Britain. Half a dozen are common enough for you to see. They have different colours and are of different sizes but their shapes are the same so you can make a number of outline drawings to colour in when you make your observations.

Bumble-bees are bigger than honey-bees. The largest queens have buff tails and are almost 3cm long. Bumble-bees have four wings, like all bees, and like other insects they have six legs. Their bodies are divided into three parts – head, thorax and abdomen. On their heads are two antennae for scenting flowers. Their long tongues can reach down into flowers for nectar and pollen. In the process, they carry pollen on their hairy bodies from the male parts of one flower to the female parts of another and fertilise them. This is essential if the plants are to continue and for this reason bumble-bees are protected in some countries of Europe.

Their life story is very strange. In the winter, the queens hibernate in dry places and come out later in the spring. The eggs, already fertilised, are held in their bodies over the winter. Immediately they look for places to build their nests. As soon as they begin to feed they build cells of wax where they lay up to twenty eggs. In other cells they store honey for the grubs to eat as they hatch. And in a couple of weeks they emerge as small worker bees. At once they go out foraging for more food while the queens lay another batch of eggs. This is continued until the nest contains a hundred or more workers. By now it is late summer and these eggs hatch into males called 'drones', or into new queens. The males and new queens do not go out foraging at all. They wait until a sunny day when the queens fly high into the sky where they are followed by the drones. The strongest drones find the queens and mate with them in the air.

Eventually the new queens seek out places to hibernate for the next winter. You may see the old queens crawling off quietly to die but the workers and the drones, too, will die before the winter.

Bumble-bees can sting in defence. So be careful not to frighten them!

Herring gulls

You will see and hear herring gulls on the seashore but they also live inland. Gulls have increased greatly in number and many now live and breed near the rubbish dumps of large towns. Perhaps the noisiest and most active are the herring gulls. Adults are white with pale grey backs, bright yellow beaks and pinkish legs. And on the beak is a red spot. But young birds up to four years old are hard to identify. Like all young gulls they have mottled brown feathers.

Herring gulls are active scavengers and will eat almost anything, even robbing other gulls if they can. But fish are their natural prey along with eggs and young birds or small animals. On the rubbish dumps, they eat waste human food, mice and rats. But those living by rocky coasts have learned how to break open shellfish by dropping them on the rocks.

Male and female herring gulls living on the shore pair up at sea whilst land birds pair up on reservoirs or lakes. They join colonies to nest on cliffs or on waste ground. The noise can be deafening! One parent must remain by the nest all the time or its neighbours would eat the eggs or even the chicks!

To get food the chicks peck at the parents' red beak spots and this makes the birds bring up the food in their stomachs for them. Herring gulls are strong fliers. They can also glide on the wind most beautifully. Sometimes they attack other birds such as terns or avocets.

Getting to know the different gulls is fun on a seaside holiday. If you have their outlines ready in your field notebook you can add the details for each and increase your list. You can see some of them in towns, too, if you look out for them.

Sand dunes

Sandy beaches form wherever the wind and sea pile sand directly against the shore. The wind then blows sand further inland until it is obstructed in some way. It settles as sand dunes. More dunes form against the old ones so that the oldest dunes are those farthest inland. Sea couch grass and marram grass collect sand as it blows. They have long roots which collect moisture and bind the dune together. Their leaves curl up in dry weather and open in the rain. Many other special plants are able to live on sand dunes. Sea hollies are low, blue-grey shrubs with prickly leaves. They have thick skins to keep in the moisture. White burnet roses grow up to a metre tall and are thickly covered in spines.

In damper places between the dunes there may be sand sedge with triangular stems or sea purslane with fleshy leaves to hold moisture. Sea peas which look like small sweet pea plants grow near the sea. Yellow poppies with fruits like long horns and little hawkweeds grow further back where a thin skin of soil has formed on the sand. Sea bindweed creeps everywhere.

Animals which feed on the plants come to the dunes. So they are good places to look for migrant butterflies such as red admirals or painted ladies which come down to rest and sip nectar after their sea crossings. Spiders trap sand flies and snails may creep up plant stems to escape the dryness of the sand. Sand lizards suddenly appear from their holes. On certain protected dunes natterjack toads survive but they are rare in our country. In the early morning, if the sand is wet, you might like to look for the tracks of mice, lizards or even snakes and foxes. These can be drawn in your field notebook to help you remember your holiday.

There are many fine coastal birds to spot such as the terns (*see below*), ringed plovers and oyster-catchers with their red beaks.

Rock pools

Rockpools are surely the most exciting habitats at the seaside! Some are tiny whilst others are large and they may even be deep enough to swim in. All are to be found between high and low tide marks so they are refilled each day by the sea. They are fun to explore – but do be careful won't you? Always watch out for the tide!

The plants and animals in rockpools may suffer if they are disturbed so it is best to watch patiently. If you turn stones over it is only fair to replace them the right way up quickly!

The big picture shows what you may find. Seaweeds are algae and are rather simple plants that do not form flowers. You should find green, red and brown seaweeds.

One brown seaweed growing on the rocks below high water mark is called bladder wrack. In the picture, you can see the tiny bladders of air that keep it floating. Larger brown seaweeds live in deeper water – great forests of wrack go down to about 30 metres. Below that there is not enough light for them to grow. Green and red seaweeds live in shallower water and other plants you are likely to see are lichens. These are often flat patches of colour on rocks or shells usually above the high water mark.

You may think that the pink 'flower' near the bottom of the picture is a plant. In fact, it is an animal although it is called a sea anemone. The small picture shows an anemone grasping a shrimp which it will eat and digest. Rockpools contain many animals and you may find crabs or even a lobster with their heavy armour of shell. Both have ten legs, eight for walking and two with pincers. There are many different colours and sizes of crabs even down to tiny ones only 1cm across.

Hermit crabs make their homes in large periwinkle or old whelk shells. They have to protect their soft bodies because they can grow armour only on their front parts. The small rounded, twisted shells you find will be other periwinkles. Orange ones graze on microscopic algae or seaweeds and breathe water with gills. The black ones have simple lungs to breathe air and they graze on lichens.

The large conical shells fastened tight to the rocks are limpets and hold on by suction. When the tide covers them they move around grazing upon the algae which live on the rocks. The much smaller shell-like cones are barnacles which begin life as free-swimming larvae in the sea. They eventually settle on rocks and undergo changes to grow shells with small holes at the top. Through these they put out feelers and feed on microscopic creatures called plankton.

'Double' shells include black mussels. The animals inside feed by drawing in water and filtering from it oxygen and tiny bits of food. They are stuck fast on the rocks by their narrow ends in great mussel beds below the high water mark.

Some small fish may remain in the pools between the tides.

In your field notebook you can make fascinating records of what you find in rockpools.

Under the sea

On holiday you may get a chance to go to sea. From a small boat you may see shoals of mackerel coming close to the shore in summer. These fast swimming fish catch much smaller creatures in the sea called plankton. The oceans of the world are full of animal and plant plankton which float in the currents. The tiny, floating plant plankton absorb the energy from sunlight which passes into the upper layers of the sea. In their turn they are fed on by the larger animal plankton. Then along come fishes like herring and mackerel to feed on them!

This is the beginning of a food chain in nature: plant plankton ⟶ animal plankton ⟶ mackerel. One creature feeds upon another. But is the mackerel at the end of the chain? Unfortunately, it is not! The mackerel may fall victim to a larger fish such as a cod or a shark. So the complete food chain might read: plant plankton ⟶ animal plankton ⟶ mackerel ⟶ cod.

The chain can be taken one stage further. You can add man!

Without plankton, the small floating plants and animals of the sea, all marine life would perish. Some of them even go to feed the largest animal ever to live in our planet – the blue whale. This feeds on shoals of krill which are small, shrimp-like creatures.

Even when they die a natural death plankton are of great value as food. Their dead bodies continually fall to the bottom of the oceans where they may be eaten by strange fishes living in the deeps.

In the picture, you can see some of the animals which live in the seas off our British coasts. At the surface are the jelly-fish which move in a fascinating way. They change shape as they pump themselves through the water. Shoals of fish may be seen near to the surface at certain times of the year – here you see mackerel, silvery pout and blue whiting.

On the seabed you will find three other fish – skate, plaice and dogfish. Can you identify each one? Plaice do not swim very much but remain camouflaged on the bottom. Also at the bottom are queen scallop, sponges, sea anemones and a lobster.

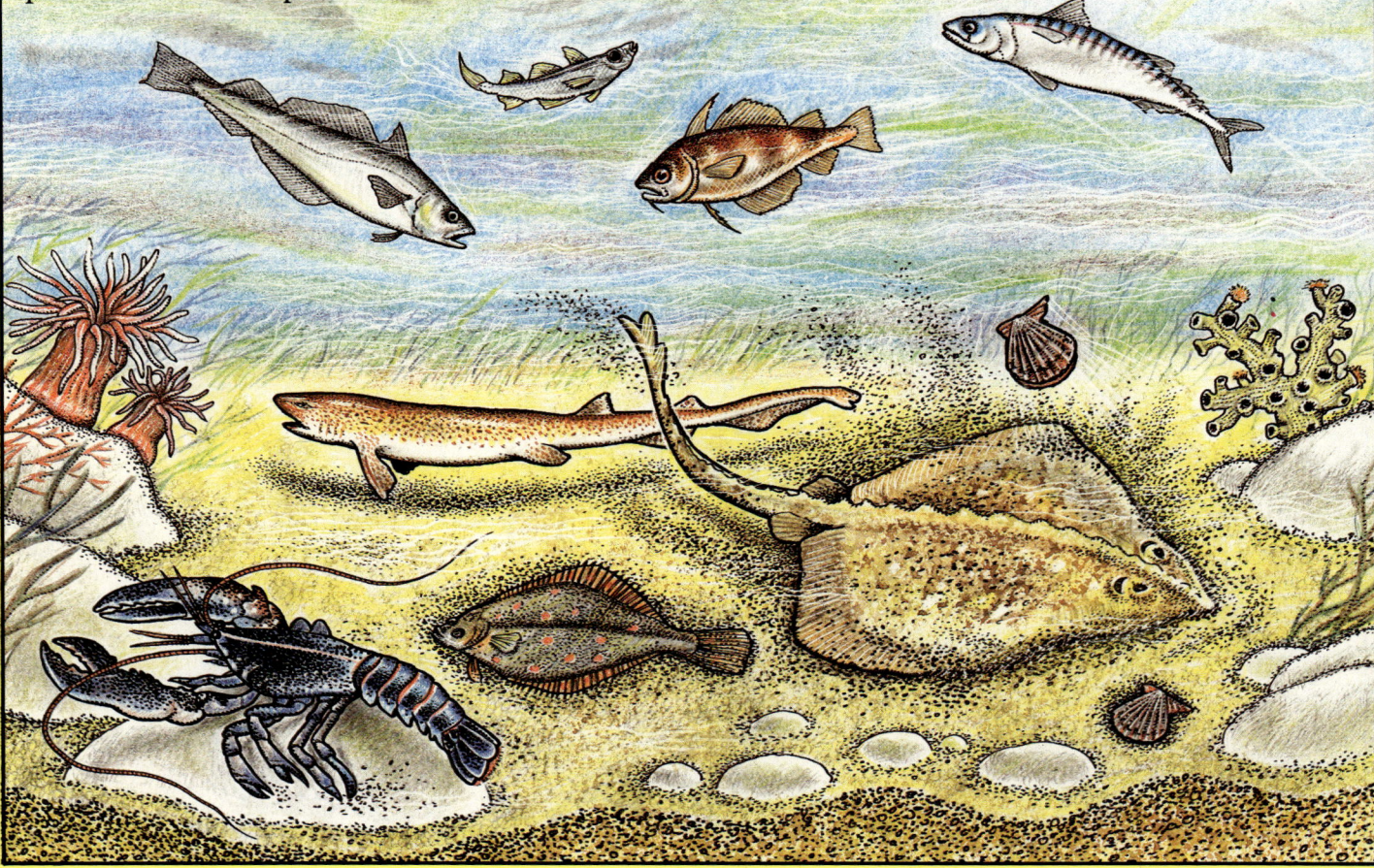